HARDY

A BEGINNER'S GUIDE

ROB ABBOTT AND CHARLIE BELL

Series Editors

Rob Abbott & Charlie Bell

Hodder & Stoughton

A MEMBER OF THE HODDER HEADLINE GROUP

Orders: please contact Bookpoint Ltd, 39 Milton Park, Abingdon, Oxon OX14 4TD. Telephone: (44) 01235 400400, Fax: (44) 01235 400500. Lines are open from 9.00–6.00, Monday to Saturday, with a 24-hour message answering service. Email address: orders@bookpoint.co.uk

British Library Cataloguing in Publication Data
A catalogue record for this title is available from The British Library

ISBN 0 340 80036 4

First published 2001
Impression number   10 9 8 7 6 5 4 3 2 1
Year 2005 2004 2003 2002 2001

Illustrations by Steve Coots.
Cover image supplied by Corbis Images
Typeset by Transet Limited, Coventry, England.
Printed in Great Britain for Hodder & Stoughton Educational, a division of Hodder Headline Plc, 338 Euston Road, London NW1 3BH by Cox & Wyman, Reading, Berks.

CONTENTS

How To Use This Book

The *Beginner's Guide* literature series aims to introduce readers to the major writers of the past 500 years. It is assumed that readers will begin with little or no knowledge and will want to go on to explore Hardy in other ways.

BEGIN READING THE AUTHOR

This book is a companion guide to Hardy's major works, it is not a substitute for reading the books themselves. It would be useful if you read at least one of Hardy's works in parallel, so that you can put theory into practice. The book is divided into sections. After considering how to approach the author's work and a brief biography, we go on to explore some of the main writings and themes before examining some critical approaches to the author. The survey finishes with suggestions for further reading and possible areas of further study.

HOW TO APPROACH UNFAMILIAR OR DIFFICULT TEXTS

Coming across a new writer may seem daunting, but do not be put off. The trick is to persevere. Much good writing is multi-layered and complex. It is precisely this diversity and complexity that makes literature rewarding and exhilarating.

Literature needs to be read more than once and in different ways. These ways can include: a leisurely and superficial reading to get the main ideas and narrative; a slower more detailed reading focusing on the nuances of the text, concentrating on what appear to be key passages; and reading in a random way, moving back and forth through the text to examine such things as themes, narrative or characterization. Undoubtedly the best way to extract the most from a text is to read it several times.

When it comes to tackling difficult words or concepts it is often enough to guess in context on the first reading, making a more detailed study using a dictionary or book of critical concepts on later reading. If you prefer to look up unusual words as you go along, be careful that you do not disrupt the flow of the text and your concentration.

USING BIOGRAPHICAL MATERIAL

Opinions differ about whether it is useful to know something of a writer's life and times before reading a text. It can certainly be fascinating to know something about an author. The information gleaned can be illuminating but it can also be irrelevant and misleading and should be treated with caution. It might be that the author wishes us to engage primarily with the text itself which is usually offered to the public with little meaningful biographical content. It should be possible with most authors to enjoy their work without knowing anything about them.

VOCABULARY

Key terms and unfamiliar words are set in **bold** text. These words are defined and explained in the glossary to be found at the back of the book. We have also summarized each section in our 'summary' sections at the end of each chapter.

You can read this introductory guide in its entirety or dip in wherever suits you. You can read it in any order. It is a tool to help you appreciate a key figure in literature. We hope you find it useful.

✳✳✳✳SUMMARY ✳✳✳✳

To maximize the use of this book:

- Read the author's work.

- Read it several times in different ways.

- Be open to innovative or unusual forms of writing.

- Treat biographical information with care and deal mainly with the texts themselves.

Rob Abbott and Charlie Bell

Why Read Hardy Today?

STILL POPULAR

The works of Thomas Hardy are very much with us today. All of his novels and most of his short stories remain in print, his *Selected Poems* still sell in large numbers and his novels have been the subject of both television and screen adaptations. This popularity may appear odd for a man whose prose has sometimes been characterized as overblown and tedious, whose plots have been criticized as contrived and dependent upon extraordinary coincidence, and whose dominant mood seems to be one of deep pessimism. And yet there is something compelling about his work and reading: it is a richly rewarding experience.

A PROVOCATIVE WRITER

Hardy was often at odds with the accepted views of his own society and came to conclude that some of his novels were ahead of their time. Hence, perhaps, their continued appeal to our own era. His desire to explore the world through his distinctive brand of **realism** often led him towards stories and themes which were seemingly not to the taste of society as a whole. Many of his novels were **bowdlerized** when they first appeared in serialized form to protect the sensibilities of the readership.

The hostile reception given to two of his last novels, *Tess of the d'Urbervilles* and *Jude the Obscure*, illustrated a growing rift between novelist and public. *Jude* was banned from public libraries and even publicly burnt to ashes by a bishop. Both novels stirred a huge outcry, particularly from those who felt him to be immoral and perverted. This reaction caused Hardy much pain: he felt misunderstood. After the reaction to *Jude*, Hardy concentrated solely on his poetry, commenting in a later postscript to the novel that the effect of this adverse publicity was to cure him of further interest in novel writing. Many critics and biographers prefer to see Hardy as essentially a poet who produced novels until wealth freed him to pursue his favoured career as a poet. This also appears to have been Hardy's view of the situation.

AHEAD OF HIS TIME

Hardy spanned the nineteenth and twentieth centuries.

Although often thought of as a Victorian, Hardy lived until 1928 and saw hugely disruptive societal changes in a long life that straddled the nineteenth and twentieth centuries. He began life in a society where Napoleon was still alive in memory, where the majority of journeys were conducted either on foot or by horse and carriage; he ended his days travelling across Europe by motor car in the unsettled times between the two major world wars of the twentieth century. Certainly the theme of change is central to his work. Often such change is seen as being detrimental to the individual, for example the extinction of old crafts and practices. The conflicting demands of accelerating change and progress would seem to have a direct link into the modern consciousness.

Similarly, the modern reader finds sympathy with Hardy's preoccupation with social injustice, something particularly prevalent in the later novels. There was the hypocritical straightjacket of Victorian morality, which trapped people and destroyed their lives; there was increasing industrialization which drove the huge forces of change in all areas of society and led to widespread disruption and distress. All of this Hardy set against the physical, social and intellectual landscapes of the day. In particular, the physical landscape dominates his novels, setting their mood, defining their psychological effects and colouring the perspectives of all touched by them.

Often his characters demonstrate strong aspirations and compulsive inner drives: this makes them interesting and appealing to a generation raised on the credo of individual freedom.

It is the metaphorical aspects of his work, and the psychological approach he took to such characters as Michael Henchard in *The Mayor of Casterbridge*, or Sue Bridehead in *Jude*, that makes him a link from **Romanticism** to **Modernism**.

KEY TERMS

Romanticism: A movement in Britain and Europe roughly between 1770 and 1848. In literary terms it emphasized self-expression and the value of individual experience, along with a strong sense of the transcendental. The motif of the movement was 'imagination' and it put forward a belief in the close links between Man and Nature. The movement is characterized by such writers as Rousseau, Wordsworth, Mary Wollstonecraft, Coleridge, Byron and Shelley.

Modernism: In literature, a broad movement of writers including T.S. Eliot, Pound, Joyce, Woolf, Yeats and D.H. Lawrence. It was informed by the works of Freud and was characterized by a persistent experimentation with language and form. Stream of consciousness is one of its major techniques, as well as dependence upon poetic image and myth.

LINKS WITH THE PAST AND THE LAND

Hardy is good at reconnecting us with our heritage and its roots in the land. His rural vision gives us a picture of his mythical Wessex as a still largely undeveloped area with few urban centres. By linking us with our heritage in this way Hardy taps into a deep instinct within us, a subconscious connection with our forbears and a consciousness of our own past.

REALISM AND MODERNISM

The dominant mode of Hardy's writing is often regarded as an intense pessimism and gloomy despair. Seen differently, Hardy was trying to be a realist, a man who saw life as it really was. Life was not something that could be borne lightly. It involved suffering whether its protagonists liked it or not, and its imperfections were what informed human life. In this sense, Hardy was right in believing that his works were ahead of his time. In a television trailer of today, we would understand what we were about to see if we were promised a 'gritty drama'. We would be being offered something that reflected the lives of 'real' or 'ordinary' people. We would not expect happy endings, we might even expect to be disturbed, to have our values and attitudes challenged. These were not the expectations of the readership of *Murray's Magazine* or the *Graphic*, nor of a society still dominated by a very conservative Christianity.

Hardy replied to his critics by saying: 'As to pessimism. My motto is, first diagnose the complaint – in this case human ills – and ascertain the cause: then set about a remedy.' (*Life* p.383).

It is the tensions between realism and Hardy's experiments with some essentially modernist techniques that make him interesting to modern readers. This will be examined in more detail later.

USE OF LANGUAGE

Hardy loved the English language. On a good day his prose showed the poet underneath and some of his descriptions can be breathtaking. His genius is perhaps best demonstrated in *Tess of the d'Urbervilles* where he mixes many lyrical passages with moments of profound psychological change and insight.

LOVE AND DEATH

Having lost his faith in his early twenties, Hardy regarded himself as an agnostic, a position which put him into direct conflict with the increasingly devout Christian faith of Emma, his first wife. Without an omniscient God to explain the world, Hardy developed a strong sense of **fatalism**, linked directly with his feelings about the environment and the frailties of human beings. Love was seen by him as a powerful force, but one which often led to misunderstandings, pain and even death. His relationship with his wife Emma was frequently turbulent and, towards the end of her life, even hostile. Yet after her death, Hardy wrote what many consider to be his finest poetry as he sought to find a way of coping with guilt and loss.

> **KEY TERM**
>
> Fatalism: The belief that all things are determined by Fate.

HARDY AND WOMEN

After he died, Hardy's second wife Florence destroyed many of his private papers. Thus a great deal of information about him was lost and the Hardy legend must remain largely enigmatic. Much of Hardy's material can be seen to have come out his relationships with women. There was his first love, Tryphena Sparks, his first wife, Emma and his second wife, Florence. There is also a largely unknown number of other women with whom he seems to have developed infatuations, but we shall never know whether these remained purely platonic. Hardy's fictional women are nearly always the instruments of change, even when subject to the whims of Fate themselves. Often they seem ethereal, naïve, too good for themselves, as Tess Durbeyfield in *Tess* or Sue Bridehead in *Jude*. Other times they are debased, worldly and manipulating, as in Arabella Donn in *Jude*.

By creating women who were both inside and outside accepted norms, he directly challenged the assumptions, and thus the sensibilities, of Victorian England. In the later poetry, there is a strong tendency towards idealization. Hardy was driven by a desire to examine the role of women in relationships and in society. His often independent heroines, based as they were in the hurly burly of a largely rural, working-class England, foreshadow the major change in the roles of women in the twentieth century. Hardy's heroines sometimes become more than we might expect of them thus contrasting with Hardy's observation that married life broadens a man and narrows a woman.

LIVING CHARACTERS

One main reason for Hardy's popular success has always been his striking characterizations. There is Sergeant Troy, Farmer Boldwood and Bethsheba Everdene struggling with their love triangle in *Far from the Madding Crowd*; Michael Henchard, racked by guilt and intemperance in *The Mayor of Casterbridge*; Tess Durbeyfield, a victim of her own verdant fecundity in *Tess*; and Jude Fawley in *Jude*, seemingly thwarted at every turn. These and a host of major and minor characters make for a wealth of interest.

✳ ✳ ✳ ✳SUMMARY ✳ ✳ ✳ ✳

We should read Hardy today because:

- He was ahead of his time in examining social and psychological issues.

- He straddled Romanticism and Modernism.

- He links us with our heritage.

- His exploration of change, particularly rural change, matches current preoccupations.

- He satirized hypocrisy and the stifling constraints of conventional morality.

- He explores male–female relationships and champions female issues.

- He created vibrant, interesting characters.

Biography

A MAN WHO CARED

> When the present has latched its postern behind my tremulous stay,
> And the May month flaps its glad green leaves like wings,
> Delicate filmed as new-spun silk, will the neighbours say,
> 'He was a man who used to notice such things'?

As the start of this poem 'Afterwards' suggests, Hardy was a man who cared deeply both about how he was seen by the public and how he would be remembered by posterity. So deeply felt was this concern that before he died he wrote an 'approved biography' which was published in the name of his second wife, Florence Hardy. That it was accepted as a genuine biography for three decades after his death shows this attempt to control history had at least a partial success. Other biographers have managed to uncover some truths hidden by this original account of Hardy's life, a process hampered by Florence's destruction of his many private papers.

EARLY YEARS AND FORMATIVE EXPERIENCES

Hardy was born on 2 June 1848 in Upper Bockhampton, a small village just outside Dorchester in Dorset. His father Thomas was a master mason and his mother Jemima had been a cook for a local clergyman. By all accounts Thomas was a fragile and unhealthy child for most of his childhood. It was during this childhood, however, that his love of the traditional was established though the stories of rural life told to him by his father. The major formative relationship during this period was with Horace Moule, the son of the Vicar of St George's, Fordington. This was a friendship that was to last until Moule's suicide in Cambridge in 1873.

Two other significant factors are worth noting about this time. They both appear to have had an impact on his developing psyche. The first was as a young child when he had a very intense relationship (Martin Seymour-Smith, in his biography *Hardy*, calls it an 'affair') with Mrs Julia Augustus Martin, the wife of a local landowner. According to the *Life*, 'she had been accustomed to take him in her lap and kiss him until he was quite a big child.' There can be no doubt that there was a sexual charge to this relationship and also in the *Life* Hardy talks of the 'thrilling "frou frou" of her four gray silk flounces'. The exact nature of this close relationship will never be known but echoes of it are to be found in the numerous intense liaisons he formed with women over his life and, of course, in his novels.

The second experience which appears to have haunted him throughout his life took place on 9 August 1856 when, aged sixteen he witnessed the hanging of one Martha Brown. The incident left him with mixed feelings: there was the deep shock of the hanging itself but there was also a strong sexual fascination as he watched the corpse swing. In a letter to Lady Pinney, recorded by Seymour-Smith, Hardy remembers the fine figure that Martha displayed, 'the tight black silk gown set off her shape as she wheeled round and back'. (Martin Seymour-Smith, *Hardy* (Bloomsbury, 1994) p.33) The event, and its disturbing implications, was to be recreated albeit at a distance, in *Tess* when the heroine, very much in the Martha Brown mould, swings from the gallows at Wintoncester.

After attending school in Dorchester, Hardy was apprenticed to John Hicks, a local architect. Six years later he moved to London where he worked for another architect, Arthur Blomfield who designed and restored churches. It is possible that he became engaged to Eliza Nicholls, a lady's maid. It is also thought likely that Hardy had a succession of obsessions with his cousins, the Sparks sisters, the most serious of which was with the youngest, Typhena Sparks, to whom he may have even given his ring. These were the first of a series of relationships with women including an unconsummated affair with Mrs Arthur Hemiter which began in 1893.

EMMA GIFFORD

In 1868 the young Thomas Hardy undertook a professional visit to St Juliot's Church near Boscastle in Cornwall where he met and fell in love with the rector's daughter, Emma Gifford. Their early relationship seems to have been passionate. Emma is reported to have been impetuous, charming, even seductive. She was certainly, at least in part, the model for Elfride Swancourt in *A Pair of Blue Eyes*. They married in September 1874. Emma was socially Hardy's superior and in the early days they appear to have shared a great deal. She acted as his research assistant, copying and updating his somewhat obsessive notebook of extracts from newspapers and books, and even at times acting as his amanuensis. Sadly for them both their relationship was slowly to change.

Emma has often been cast as a dull, unattractive burden to be borne with increasing irritation by Hardy the creative genius. This would seem unfair. Many reports suggest she was in reality far from dull and even had her own literary gifts as her early magazine articles and unpublished travel diaries show. Whatever her faults, the relationship quickly fell apart. There were a few very good years. Their blissful time living at Sturminster Newton was later to be described by Hardy as 'a preface without a book'. What had started with such promise soon fizzled into a distant and estranged relationship. The change began after they moved to south London, a move designed to further Hardy's career. Such furtherance was soon achieved and within a short space of time the still very shy and reserved Hardy had a circle of acquaintances which included Thomas Huxley, the publisher Alexander Macmillan and the actor Henry Irving. While Hardy was enjoying his new life Emma increasingly found herself left behind. That her looks had faded was another factor in the decline of their relationship. Whether Hardy was ever physically unfaithful to her is the subject of much futile speculation.

He began a series of infatuations with beautiful women, starting with a young actress named Helen Matthews. A serious illness then convinced Hardy that London was bad for his health and in 1881 the Hardys moved back to Dorset, first taking a house at Wimbourne and then finally in 1885 moving to a house he had designed himself, Max Gate, just outside Dorchester.

In May 1983 Hardy and Emma visited Ireland where Hardy met Florence Henniker. Hardy was immediately attracted to her, or at least to the idea of her. Although the evidence is scarce he does seem to have pursued her with some persistence, although her married state and beliefs in fidelity prevented it ever becoming more than a very close friendship. This seems to have been the pattern with a number of women including Mary Jeune and Agnes Groves.

FLORENCE DUGDALE

In 1906 Hardy, then in his late fifties, met Florence Dugdale. She was a self-professed admirer of Hardy. Thus began a relationship which was to be both deep and intimate, although again the evidence suggests it may never have been a fully sexual one. Surprisingly Florence and Emma seem to have got on reasonably well, although the fearful arguments between Hardy and his increasingly estranged wife were to prove very difficult for Florence.

DEATH OF EMMA

After a period of illness, Emma's health deteriorated rapidly during the latter part of 1912. Her refusal to acknowledge her own ill health, and a complete breakdown of her relationship with Hardy, meant that her condition went undiagnosed and untreated. On 27 November 1912 she died in her room from what was afterwards certified as impacted gall-stones and heart failure.

That Hardy felt deep remorse and regret for his behaviour towards Emma is testified by the rush of poems about her and their early relationship which followed her death. Despite the confused emotions following her death, Hardy had proposed marriage to Florence Dugdale by April of 1913 and they were married the following February.

OLD AGE

The outbreak of war greatly depressed Hardy. Despite the attentions of a young wife he had by now become very set in his ways. There were, however, happier moments, for example, the honorary degree from Oxford University (the Christminster of *Jude*). Life seems to have been peaceful and orderly in his later years, allowing him time to write poetry and complete the autobiography written as if by Florence. Hardy died in 1928, by then a great man. The pall bearers at his funeral included other great men of his age: J.M. Barrie, John Galsworthy, Rudyard Kipling and George Bernard Shaw. His heart was buried at Stinsford churchyard next to Emma while the rest of his body is buried at Poet's Corner, Westminster, alongside that other great author, Charles Dickens.

✳ ✳ ✳ ✳SUMMARY ✳ ✳ ✳ ✳

- Hardy was a man who cared deeply about how he was perceived.

- His formative influences included a close relationship with a much older woman and seeing a hanging.

- His marriage to Emma Gifford began with great happiness but soon deteriorated to one of mere sufferance.

- Hardy had a number of obsessive but probably platonic relationships with other women.

- After his wife's death he suffered from tremendous remorse.

- He is buried in Poet's Corner alongside Dickens.

3 Social and Historical Background

Hardy was writing and publishing novels from the late 1860s until the late 1890s and publishing his poetry from then until the 1920s. The novels themselves were often set within a slightly earlier period from the 1800s onwards. Thus his writing covers a huge span of over a hundred years. In historical terms it stretches from the defeat of Napoleon at Waterloo until the First World War. This vast period was also an era of huge social and political change.

SHIFT OF POPULATION

One such change was in the shift and growth of the population, mostly from the country into the developing towns and cities, but also overseas to the new colonies and the New World. One example will suffice. In 1801 the population of London was just over one million, by 1851 it was 2.5 million, by 1901 it was 6.5 million. This was a truly astonishing rise and was reflected in other cities around the country with the countryside feeling the attendant effects of an ever-dwindling population.

SOCIAL CLASS

Social class and the distinction between classes was a key theme for Hardy. Stephen Smith is barred from marrying Elfride Swancourt in *A Pair of Blue Eyes* because he comes from humble origins. Similarly Dr Edred Fitzpiers is preferred to the rural and lowly Giles Winterbourne in *The Woodlanders*. This theme is explored in other ways in *Tess* and *Jude* and many other novels.

In 1873 four-fifths of the land was owned by less than seven thousand people. Thus a very small class of highly privileged, very rich men, formed the social elite in England. There was also a rising middle class who aspired to the privileges and status of their aristocratic betters. Many Victorian novelists including Hardy, Dickens and George Eliot explore the tension arising from the rise of this highly aspirational middle class.

In terms of the rural England, which is the setting for almost all of Hardy's novels, there were three main ranks in the social and economic structure. First there were the landowners, referred to above, then there was a class of tenant farmers and finally a class of landless labourers.

This was the dominant pattern but not the only one: there was still a class who were 'small-holders' and alongside these what Hardy describes as 'an interesting and better informed class' which includes what we might refer to as tradesmen such as shoe-makers and smiths. The Durbeyfield family in *Tess* and the Winterbourne family in *The Woodlanders* are life-holders entitled to their cottages for only three generations. There is also the pressure from a developing urban economy where traditional skills are being replaced by mechanization and mass production. Hardy himself was born into such an intermediate family.

COUNTRY AND CUSTOM
The nineteenth century was also a time when England was a very powerful nation. The Industrial Revolution was in full swing, converting a largely rural economy into an industrial world power. The novels of Thomas Hardy provide a commentary on one aspect of this revolution – the effect it had on the countryside. Hardy largely laments the course of such progress, seeing the changes in England as detrimental. He decries the death of custom and tradition and in novels such as *The Woodlanders* and *Under the Greenwood Tree* we are often shown customs which even at the time of writing had all but died out.

A passage from *Tess* serves to show Hardy's feelings about the dehumanizing effect of mechanization in agriculture. In Chapter 47, we find Tess acting as part of a team, dismantling a straw rick and feeding a large, noisy and hungry threshing machine, the sort of machine which was often the target of **Luddite**-style protests.

The machine is described in terms of the oppression it exerts on the workforce with its 'despotic demand upon the endurance of their muscles and nerves'. Attending the steam engine which drives the thresher is a curious being who is described at some length. He is 'the sooty and grimy embodiment of tallness, in a sort of trance, with a heap of coals by his

side.' He is described in terms of his isolation from the other workers and also from the rural life in which he has come to work:

> What he looked he felt. He was in the agricultural world, but not of it.
> He served fire and smoke; these denizens of the field (the farm workers)
> served vegetation, weather, frost and sun.

His isolation and alienation from the other workers is heightened when we learn that he speaks with a northern accent and travels from 'farm to farm, from county to county.' He has little intercourse with the farm workers 'as if some ancient doom compelled him to wander here against his will in the service of his Plutonic master.' Hardy's description of the new alienation is completed by reporting how the man would describe himself to the farm labourers, not as a farm worker but as 'an engineer', someone dealing with mechanisms rather than the vagaries of human, animal and vegetable life.

TRANSPORT AND DISTANCE

Another feature of Victorian England was the incredible expansion in mobility occasioned by the spread of the railways. The rate of development of the railways is phenomenal: the first railway from London to Manchester was begun in 1830 and by 1850 there were over 6,000 miles of track connecting towns across England. Movement from town to town, or country to town, had previously been very difficult, indeed in the winter it was often impossible. Journeys by coach and horse were long and uncomfortable. The railways transformed this and did so in a remarkably short time.

Distance, and the effect of transportation on human life, are made great play of in Hardy's work. Vast distances were being tamed in the early nineteenth century by the railways and this contrasts with the fact that most journeys were being made on foot, on horse or by some form of cart or carriage. The contrast of travelling styles is often highlighted by Hardy. In *Tess*, Tess and Angel take their locally produced milk by horse and trap to the station so that it can be carried to the great metropolis of London. In *A Pair of Blue Eyes* it is the speed of the train from Plymouth to London which allows Elfride and Smith to travel to London and back in one day, although she has travelled to Plymouth on horseback. Travel on foot was still commonplace: in *Jude*, the quack doctor, Dr Vilbert, travels vast distances through Wessex every week on foot, moving at a fast, jogging pace.

SEX AND SEXUALITY

A consistent theme in Hardy's novels is innocence, a euphemism for virginity. Many of the stories revolve around the keeping or the losing of this innocence as well as wider questions of fidelity and morality. Single women were expected to remain 'pure' and the social penalties for not doing so remained severe.

Sex and sexuality were unspoken topics, furtive and shameful even towards the end of the nineteenth century. Hardy's novels were shocking not only because they dared to explore sexual issues but also because they implied approval for behaviour which broke a very strict moral code. His characters dared to question the conventional moral stance on topics such as marriage and fidelity.

Women particularly were barred from public discussion of sexual matters. There was for many a complete denial that women had a sexuality at all, as this extract from William Acton's *The Functions and*

Disorders of the Reproductive Organs published in successive editions from 1857 to 1862 shows:

> As a general rule, a modest woman seldom desires any sexual gratification for herself. She submits to her husband but only to please him; and but for the desire of maternity, would far rather be relieved from his attentions.
>
> Cited in Boumelha, P. *Thomas Hardy and Women: Sexual Ideology and Narrative Form* (Harvester, 1982) p.14

Where women do express sexual feelings in Hardy's novels it tends to be expressed in such euphemistic terms that the modern reader may pass it unawares. For example, in *The Woodlanders* Fitzpiers is said to exercise a 'strange influence' over Grace. This is referred to elsewhere in the novel as an 'intoxication'. Similarly it is often hard to fathom the effect the dastardly Alec d'Urberville has on Tess, even if it is impossible to understand her actions without acknowledging that she feels a strong sexual attraction to him.

HARDY AND MORALITY

For a man who seems to have regarded himself as a moralist, Hardy frequently found himself outside the moral parameters of his time. This is shown nowhere more clearly than in the cuts he was forced to make to his work to enable publication in serial magazines. In *Tess*, for example, both the scenes in which Alec seduces Tess were removed as was the section dealing with Tess's unconventional baptism of her illegitimate child, Sorrow. In *Jude* the cuts were even more severe. Sue and Jude were prevented from ever consummating their relationship, Jude was tricked into marriage not by Arabella pretending she was pregnant but rather by the threat that a former sweetheart wished to marry her. The whole section where Sue tells Father Time about her forthcoming baby was also cut. Looking at what was excised from *Harper's New Monthly Magazine* it is a wonder that the stories made any sense at all in their serial form!

MARRIAGE AND DIVORCE

In both *Jude* and *The Woodlanders* a registry office marriage is contemplated. The *Marriage Act* of 1836 allowed that marriages could take place in registry offices, but until then marriage had only been permissible, except by special licence, in an Anglican church.

In *Tess*, Angel Clare is seen at the end of the novel married to Liza-Lu. This marriage would in fact have been illegal until the passing of the *Deceased Wife's Sister Act* in 1907. It would also have been seen as incestuous.

It is important to remember that at this time all a woman's property and wealth passed over to her husband as soon as she married. From the beginning of the eighteenth century divorce was possible in England by getting an Act of Parliament to dissolve the marriage on the grounds of adultery. This was costly and difficult and obviously well beyond the means of any but the very wealthy. Between 1840 and 1856 only 24 such Acts were passed. The only alternative was legal separation, after which neither party could re-marry and the husband maintained the rights to his wife's property.

The *Act to Amend the Law Relative to Matrimonial Clauses in England* of 1857 changed all this. Divorce was now available through a civil court. A husband could divorce on the grounds of his wife's adultery. For the wife it was not so straight-forward. She could petition for divorce only if she could prove that her husband had been incestuous, bigamous, or guilty of rape, sodomy or bestiality. Failing any of these, she could divorce her husband on the grounds of adultery but only if this was coupled with cruelty.

HARDY AS A VICTORIAN THINKER

In some respects Hardy was very much a man of his age, and in others he was unconventional and highly radical. He was highly influenced by other radical thinkers of his era, notably Charles Darwin and John Stuart Mill. Darwin's theories on the evolution of life were first published in *Origin of the Species* in 1859. As a theory it scandalized Victorian Christian values. If life evolved as Darwin suggested then the whole biblical creation story was wrong and the certainty of even God himself was undermined. As an agnostic, Hardy was certainly influenced by such views which in turn he used, often somewhat scandalously, within his novels. When Tess, for example, descending the Egdon slopes is described as, 'like a fly on a billiard-table of indefinite length, and of no more consequence to the surroundings than that fly' (Chapter 16) we see clearly the effects of Darwin's thinking as we do when Jude and Sue question God, marriage and morality.

HARDY'S WESSEX

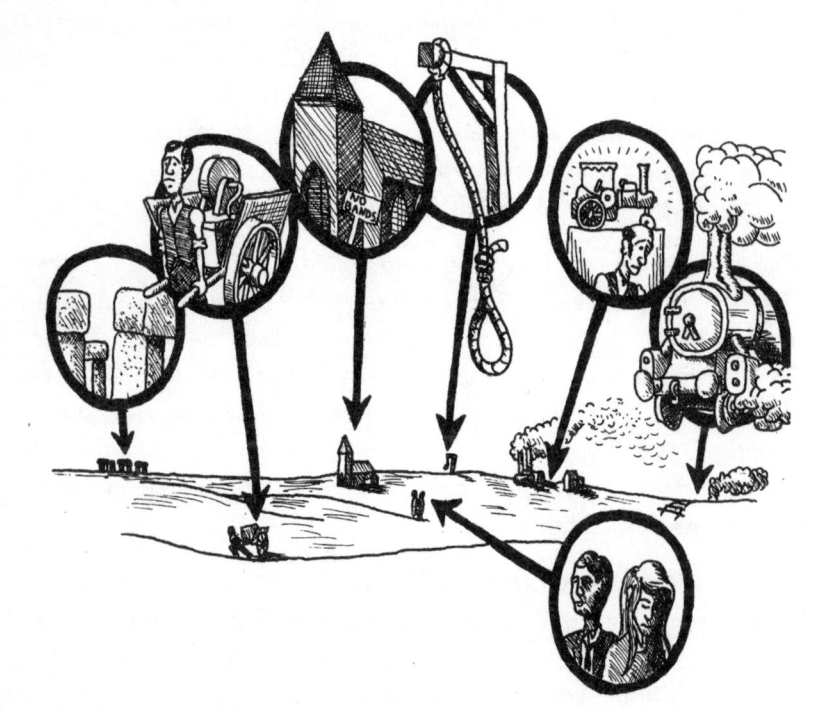

Hardy's Wessex – old style

Wessex was a place that slowly grew in Hardy's imagination. It was not until the writing of *The Mayor of Casterbridge* that it became a clearly defined region. After this the early novels were revised and made to conform to the topography of the imaginary place, ready for publication in the collected edition.

From this point onwards the novels were all set in Hardy's mythical Wessex, a place which is similar to the real southern and western part of England but which is sufficiently far removed from it to serve an allegorical purpose. Hardy did produce a map which showed the physical location of the towns and villages of Wessex and the table below shows the fictional names alongside their real world equivalences:

Bramshurst (The Great Forest)	Brockenhurst (New Forest)
Budmouth	Weymouth
Casterbridge	Dorchester
Deadman's Bay	Lyme Bay
Exonbury	Exeter (Devon)
Havenpool	Poole
Idmouth	Sidmouth (Devon)
Kingsbere	Bere Regis
Lulwind Cove	Lulworth Cove
Melchester	Salisbury (Wiltshire)
Mellstock	Stinsford
Pebble Bank	Chesil Beach
Sandbourne	Bournemouth
Stourcastle	Sturminster Newton
The Island	Isle of Wight
Warborne	Wimborne
Weatherbury	Puddletown
Wintoncester	Winchester (Hampshire)

Yet such maps and tables are very misleading. Casterbridge, is not Dorchester it is rather a fictionalized town occupying a similar space to Dorchester. The landscapes of Hardy are important within themselves for they form a psychological, moral and emotional setting for the human dramas that unfold. As Richard Taylor puts it: 'The real Hardy country is off the map and in the mind.' Richard H. Taylor, in Norman Page (ed.), *Hardy: The Writer and his Background*, (London, 1980), p.223.

* * * *SUMMARY * * * *

- Hardy lived through a period of tremendous social and political change.

- The population of large cities grew massively in part because people moved from the country to the town.

- There were great inequalities between the different social classes.

- Gender roles were highly prescribed and very restrictive for women.

- Hardy was in many ways a radical thinker but in others highly conservative.

- Hardy's novels are all set in the fictional county of Wessex.

How to Approach Hardy's Work

4

NO SPECIAL KEY REQUIRED

There is no need for a special 'key' to unlock the pleasures of Hardy's work whether it be poetry or prose. The text largely speaks for itself, and where it does not, Hardy is sure to include enough of his own thoughts to make his intentions clear.

SWITCH OFF MODERN SENSIBILITIES

One thing the modern reader is advised to do, at least at first reading, is to switch off twenty-first century sensibilities and try to enter the Victorian world presented by Hardy, remembering that he often sets his fiction in *his* near historic past. By presenting an earlier age afresh he aims to reflect some of the issues of contemporary life that absorb his interest.

Recent approaches to scholarship have meant that Hardy must inevitably be viewed in fresh ways. This book charts some of the major modern critical movements and how they approach Hardy's work. However, a first reading which pays close attention to the novels as stories is recommended before examining any literary criticism. It is important to establish your own responses before considering those of others.

SAVOUR THE WRITING

Hardy stands with Dickens as a writer who shaped his own time, and as someone who has remained popular in the public eye. Increasingly he is being revived in academic circles too.

He is a lyrical writer, a poet who engaged in the writing of novels. His style reaches near perfection in novels such as *Tess* where landscape, character and plot all fuse together to provide a transcendental experience. Take, for example, the passage which comes after Tess has baptized her ailing and illegitimate baby, Sorrow, in a touching ceremony:

> Poor Sorrow's campaign against sin, the world, and the devil was doomed to be of limited brilliancy – luckily perhaps for himself, considering his beginnings. In the blue of the morning that fragile soldier and servant breathed his last, and when the other children awoke, they cried bitterly, and begged Sissy to have another pretty baby.
>
> *Tess*, Chapter 14

Here Hardy has avoided over-sentimentality by employing irony to describe Sorrow's plight ('limited brilliancy', 'soldier and servant') and a poetic touch ('blue of the morning') which sets the death in the context of a wider world. The innocence of the children and the contrasting of 'pretty' with the baby's name Sorrow, heightens Tess's plight and contrasts her 'innocence' with theirs. On a first reading though, we are unlikely to be aware of the power of this passage (and many others) and will be beguiled by the engaging quality of the story itself.

Indeed, for some, Hardy has been regarded as a realist, writing simple and sometimes sentimental stories about country life, but it would be a mistake to regard him in this way. Hardy can be regarded as a bridge between two literary movements, the Romantics and the Modernists.

He was also experimenting with a more psychological approach to writing and fused elements together to create a rich tapestry of meanings, contradictions and ideas. In the *Life*, he writes that novel writing must develop: 'Having reached the analytic stage it must transcend it by going still further in the same direction. Why not by rendering as visible essences, spectres, &c. the abstract thoughts of the analytic school.'

We could not fully appreciate Michael Henchard in *The Mayor of Casterbridge* if we simply saw him as a moody man. Hardy was portraying a complex individual whose behaviour cannot be explained rationally and which could not be explained until the arrival of the science of psychoanalysis in the next century. Hardy's achievement was to create a central character about whom we are forced to be ambivalent and who it is difficult to judge in black and white terms.

VARIABLE QUALITY

Sometimes, Hardy wrote less than sublimely. It is interesting for example to note that *The Well-Beloved* was written between *Tess* and *Jude*, regarded as two of his finest novels, but does not carry the same critical or popular acclaim. Other works in his canon such as *A Laodicean,* and *Life's Little Ironies* are also less well known and regarded.

Readers often find some of his descriptive passages pompous and overblown, the classical references obscure and his imagery at times muddled. Here is one such example:

> Even among the moodiest, the tendency to be cheered is stronger than the tendency to be cast down; and a soul's specific gravity stands permanently less than that of the sea of troubles into which it is thrown.
>
> *The Woodlanders,* Chapter 14

Although not one of his worst, this passage with its mixed metaphor, over-complex sentence structure and the veiled reference to Shakespeare demonstrates some of Hardy's tendencies.

Hardy was writing for serialization. This meant tight deadlines or last-minute rewrites to please an editor. Often his American serializers demanded changes which were different from the British serializations and to the eventual book versions. Although Hardy was a perpetual (if not neurotic) rewriter of his work, sometimes things slipped through the net.

READING THE POEMS

Many of Hardy's poems are short and accessible. They are best read in batches, taking several poems from a particular collection and reading one poem after another. This is a slightly unusual method of approach but it does help the reader to get a feel for the moods and themes of the poems. You can then return to individual poems and examine them in more detail.

One such sequence well worth studying is entitled 'War Poems' to be found in the collection *Poems of the Past and the Present*. Here you will find poems looking at war from a variety of viewpoints (narrator, soldiers, an officer, wives and 'sweethearts') and in a variety of situations and locations. A first continuous reading of this sequence will present a kaleidoscopic view of the effects of war, in particular the separation brought about by it. Further close reading of each poem in turn will then reveal a subtlety of content, ideas, form and style.

LOOK FOR HARDY'S THEMES

Hardy saw himself as someone who could see what others, either through selfishness, dogma or lack of humanity, could not. There can be no doubt that he touched a nerve with his readership and often provoked strong reaction, much of it adverse. The themes are strong and many of them are still very relevant today as we shall see in the next chapter.

✳✳✳✳SUMMARY ✳✳✳✳

● To get the most from Hardy:

– Suspend twenty-first century sensibilities.

– Savour the writing.

– Look out for subtleties and complexities.

– Read the poetry in short batches and then return to individual poems.

– Be aware of his themes.

Major Themes

5

HARDY'S PREOCCUPATIONS

Thomas Hardy had a set of preoccupations which he returned to over and over again. Although these remained constant, the treatment of them and the emphasis put upon them changed significantly with each book or collection of poems.

In an excellent introduction to *Jude* (Everyman, 1985), J. Hillis Miller expands this idea seeing Hardy's characters as members of the same family. By using a passage from 'La Prisonnière' in Proust's *À la Recherche du Temps Perdu*, Miller goes on to argue that Hardy, like other great writers and artists such as Stendhal, Vermeer, Bonnard and Dostoyevsky, creates the same work of art over and over again in slightly different ways. He points to a passage in *Tess* where she refuses to learn history because she feels that she will discover herself to be in a long line of people who make the same mistakes repeatedly.

> ' ...what's the use of learning that I am one of a long row only – finding out that there is set down in some old book somebody just like me, and to know that I shall only act her part; making me sad, that's all. The best is not to remember that your nature and your past doings have been just like thousands' and thousands', and that your coming life and doings'll be like thousands' and thousands'.'
>
> *Tess*, Chapter 19

Miller comments:

> One of the most powerful aspects of Hardy's fiction is the way it shows characters acting freely from moment to moment, making apparently autonomous choices and decisions, and yet discovering, when they look back at their lives, ... with the kind of distance the narrator or the

reader has, that those lives fall into highly abstract patterns that seem pre-ordained.

J. Hillis Miller, *Jude The Obscure*,
(Everyman edition, 1985), Introduction xiv–xviii

There is a sense in other novels, too, that what seems like a free choice is, in reality, just another step towards a fatalistically determined future. Michael Henchard's downward journey from wealth to destitution in *The Mayor of Casterbridge* or Tess's role as sacrificial victim both seem to be examples of this pattern.

INTO HARDY – *A PAIR OF BLUE EYES*

A way of discovering the themes, one could even call them obsessions, which pervade Hardy's novels is to begin with one of his earlier works, his third published novel *A Pair of Blue Eyes*. This contains many of the elements and themes which are explored in his later works. Indeed Hardy described *A Pair of Blue Eyes* as 'feeling his way to a method'. It is a novel which is today seen as a minor work but was one much esteemed by Hardy's contemporaries, including Coventry Patmore and Tennyson, the latter holding it in higher esteem than any of Hardy's other novels.

Autobiographical influences

A Pair of Blue Eyes draws upon the young Hardy's own recent emotional history, in particular his journey to Cornwall to survey a church for renovation and his falling in love with Emma Gifford, his future wife. The character of Henry Knight bears a resemblance to Hardy's own mentor and school friend Horace Moule. There has been endless speculation about which of Hardy's acquaintances served as models for his fictional characters, particularly for his strong female characters such as Tess, Bathsheba Everdene and Sue Brideshead. The biographies by Michael Millgate or Robert Gittings are a good source for those who seek the answers (see Chapter 9 for details).

Breeding and background

A Pair of Blue Eyes begins when Stephen Smith, an architect's assistant, arrives at the vicarage in Endelstow, Cornwall to survey the church with a view to restoration. Initially, Elfride's father takes heartily to the self-taught draughtsman but turns against him when he discovers that Stephen's father is merely a humble stonemason and bricklayer who lives locally. This theme of a poor but intelligent man struggling against all odds is a motif of Hardy's work, recurring most notably in *Jude* (Jude himself) but also in *The Woodlanders* (Giles Winterbourne), and *Return of the Native* (Diggory Venn).

The plight of Victorian women

The heroine, Elfride Swancourt, is young and pretty (and just a little muddle-headed). The epigraph to Chapter 1 talks of 'a fair vestal, throned in the west'. Like many of Hardy's women, she is trapped between conventional morality on the one hand and her human desires on the other. She evades telling the truth in order to preserve her love, only to be rejected when the truth is finally revealed. In modern times, the hidden sordidness seems almost ludicrously trivial: an unchaperoned kiss, a wavering heart and a previous lover (in the non-sexual sense). Elfride, and her new stepmother, the ugly but monied Mrs Troyston, embody the plight of women in the nineteenth century. Their only hope of respectability and a decent living was to be married and the only way for women to survive outside this holy union was by deception and hypocrisy, a theme explored in *Jude* (Sue Brideshead), *Tess* (Tess), *The Woodlanders* (Grace Melbury) and *The Mayor of Casterbridge* (Lucetta Templeman) among others.

Freedom of the individual

Although not fully developed in *A Pair of Blue Eyes*, there is often an undercurrent of tension in Hardy's novels when people are thwarted in their intentions by society or social pressures. Elfride and Stephen elope to London to marry because they are opposed by her father, but they are then further thwarted by Elfride's guilt and fear of shame.

Other novels explore this idea further and it lies at the heart of *Jude*, where an individual's right to choose whom they live with and whether or not to marry them is a major concern.

Sexuality

Elfride falls in love with two men: one, Stephen Smith, being of low birth, self-taught, honest, passionate but rather weak; the other, Henry Knight, being intellectually challenging, strong but hopelessly out of touch with his feelings. The bond between Knight and Elfride is strengthened when she saves his life. In a scene which both shocked and engaged Victorian readers, she rescues him from a dramatic cliff fall by tearing up her clothes to make a rope. She is left wearing immodestly very little and, after a relieved hug with her lover, has to scurry home. This near sexual encounter, and the electric frisson it brought to the novel, is echoed somewhere in almost all the other novels: the strawberry eating scene in *Tess*; the strong sexual tensions between Grace and Fitzpiers in *The Woodlanders*; the sensuality of Bathsheba Everdene in *Far From the Madding Crowd*; and the way Sue Bridehead's frigidity is heightened by her close bodily encounters with Jude in *Jude*.

Progress

In the idyllic town of Endelstow, it may appear that time is passing by without exerting any influence. However, in Victorian England the railways were insinuating themselves ever westward, and the craze for church restoration meant the sweeping out of the old in the name of progress. In Hardy's view, the change which these events represented was often an unfeeling process leaving misery and distress in its wake. In *A Pair of Blue Eyes*, the restoration of West Endelstow church entails the demolition of the tower which, as part of the plot, results in the death of a major character and subsequent trouble for Elfride and her two lovers. The negative effects of progress are frequently highlighted in the novels, a theme established earlier in *Under The Greenwood Tree*.

UNDER THE GREENWOOD TREE

Under the Greenwood Tree is often referred to as Hardy's pastoral novel. Written in 1871, it was his first successful and popular book, enthusiastically received and still very popular today. The novel is two stories welded together. The first is the story of the Mellstock church choir and the second a love story. As such it brings together a number of familiar Hardy themes – for example, change, duplicity and rural tradition.

Change

The impact of change upon rural traditions is epitomized in this novel by the decision of Parson Maybold to replace the church choir and orchestra with a new church organ. The notion of change and progress is seen through the portrayal of three generations of the Dewy family. The sense we have here of a rural community fixed in time is created particularly in the Christmas scenes. Even at the time of writing it was a way of life severely under threat if not almost extinct. In creating the village and its community Hardy drew upon personal memory and also upon the stories he was told as a child.

Rural tradition

The trials and tribulations of the Mellstock choir is central to the novel. Even so it is hard to read now without feeling that the writing is patronizing; indeed, in the *Life* Hardy admits with some regret that what he portrayed can only be termed burlesque. The villagers are reminiscent of the 'mechanicals' in *A Midsummer Night's Dream* and the narrator seems so often to regard them in much the same way as the court of Theseus regards Bottom and his fellow tradesmen. Village life is often portrayed by Hardy in the novels and the tone seems condescending to modern taste.

Deceit and the courtship plot

Welded, not always successfully, onto the main story in *Under the Greenwood Tree* is the simple love story of Dick Dewey and Fancy Day. This story is both typical and atypical of Hardy. Like *A Pair of Blue*

Eyes, there is the theme of social inequality. Fancy Day as a school teacher is seen as socially superior to Dick. This sense of inequality is often seen as a major Hardy obsession.

Almost always this exploration of class difference is carried out with that other favoured theme, gender difference, set alongside the **courtship plot**. In using this Hardy was writing from a tradition that by the end of the nineteenth century had established itself as largely a female one. In this sense

> **KEY TERM**
>
> Courtship plot: The most basic of all stories: boy meets girl and, after overcoming a series of obstacles, they marry.

Hardy is in the tradition of Jane Austen, George Eliot and the Brontës. Courtship in every novel is central to the plot. Most of these involve a number of suitors each seeking the hand in marriage of a beautiful woman. Bathsheba Everdene is sought by Gabriel Oak, Farmer Boldwood and Sergeant Troy in *Far from the Madding Crowd*; Grace Melbury is sought by Dr Edred Fitzpiers and Giles Winterbourne in *The Woodlanders*; and, of course, Fancy Day is pursued by Dick Dewey and Parson Maybold in *Under the Greenwood Tree*.

In the latter, unlike so many others, the resolution is a happy one, or almost so at least. The last line of the novel, ' "O, 'tis a nightingale," murmured she, and thought of a secret she would never tell', serves as a epithet for much of what was to follow in Hardy's work, for the forming, keeping and breaking of secrets is central to Hardy. Many of his plots hinge on the use of deceit to hide embarrassment or to prevent loss of relationships or public respectability. The novels are peopled with characters who are in the same dilemma as Elfride, in *A Pair of Blue Eyes*, and it is so often these deceits, or withholdings of the truth, which bring about tragedy, as is famously the case in *Tess*. As we shall see later, it was in *The Mayor of Casterbridge* that this device was most effectively sustained.

'THE WITHERED ARM'

Superstition

In a famous Hardy short story, 'The Withered Arm', (*Wessex Tales*, first published 1888) we can observe the way that Hardy uses superstition and fatalism in his work. Hardy took a real story as the basis of the piece. Here, in a lush dairy-land setting, later to be expanded in *Tess*, is worked out a tale of dark, supernatural forces. Rhoda, the jilted lover of local farmer, Mr Lodge, becomes obsessed with her pretty young replacement. One night she wakes to find the **incubus** of Gertrude, Lodge's new bride, in a hideous and distorted state, sitting on her chest and bearing her down. The figure mocks her by thrusting forward her left hand to show the wedding ring. Rhoda grabs the left arm and throws off the incubus.

KEY TERM

Incubus: An evil spirit supposed to descend upon sleeping people, and often to have sexual intercourse with sleeping women. Belief in these evil creature, was widespread: indeed, the existence of such incubi was recognized by law in Medieval times. Many women claimed that their illegitimate children were the result of rape by an incubus.

The arm of the farmer's wife slowly grows withered to match that which Rhoda saw in her visitation. Rhoda is solicitous but doesn't reveal her secret. Rhoda and her son leave the area. Gertude Lodge visits Conjuror Trendle who reveals that the only way she can rid herself of the affliction is to touch the neck of a hanged man with the limb.

Although the story spans several years it seems to cover a period from spring to winter in Gertrude's life. Hardy leaves the question of superstition unanswered. The nature of the incubus is left ambiguous, but it has strong Freudian associations (in a time before the advent of psychoanalysis as a science). Also we cannot be sure whether the corpse does in fact turn Gertrude's blood, or whether she is simply overwhelmed by events. Both Gertrude and Rhoda are not in control of their lives or actions and a force stronger than themselves determines their destiny.

Hardy was fascinated by age-old superstitions.

Hardy's short stories, based as they are on real stories he had heard, are redolent of this superstition and folklore, and among others they cover subjects such as smuggling, hanging, and Napoleon's unsuccessful attempt to invade England.

Layered stories

In his longer prose, Hardy's Wessex is full of superstition, unfeeling nature, human desire, unforgiving social convention and fatalism. The novels, just like 'The Withered Arm', follow linear plot lines, but these are overlaid with onion skins of complexity. The key to full enjoyment of Hardy is to be aware of these complexities. In *Tess*, the plot of a country girl losing her virginity and suffering for it until her tragic death, is overlaid with many other layers including: the church and its teachings about conventional morality; great families fallen onto hard times and new upstart families replacing them; the role of women and their subservience to men; lies, deceit and superstition; and the fickleness of Fate. Hardy tends to work from the general to the particular, using individual human tragedies to illustrate wider social and political themes.

THE POETRY

Hardy wrote poetry throughout his life but not so copiously during his novel writing years. When he finished writing prose he began an extraordinarily prolific period of writing poems. His canon consists of nearly one thousand poems. It is as if, suddenly freed of the constraints that the novel form brings, he was able to articulate more clearly his major concerns.

In general terms, the themes of his poetry are consistent with those of the novels, concentrating much on matters of love and death, a preoccupation with the passing of time, science and religion, nature, futility, fate, sorrow, loss and regret.

'The Darkling Thrush'

Hardy's vision was not totally bleak. A mid-life poem, 'The Darkling Thrush' begins on a day of 'Winter's dregs made desolate,' when the frost is 'spectre-gray'. 'The land's sharp features seemed to be 'the Century's corpse outleant'. There doesn't seem to be much joy or fun here. Is Hardy simply wallowing in his constitutional gloominess again? If you read the whole poem carefully, you will not find this to be the case. The poem turns in the third of the four stanzas when, above 'The bleak twigs overhead,' a voice is heard. It is the voice of an aged thrush, 'frail, gaunt, and small,/In blast beruffled plume.' In spite of the potential for gloom and despair so near to the twilight of his life, the thrush chooses to 'fling his soul upon the growing gloom.' The sound is described as 'ecstatic'. Hardy muses in the final verse: 'That I could think there trembled through/His happy good-night air/Some blessed Hope, whereof he knew/And I was unaware.'

Although the poem is set in winter and the wind blows a 'death-lament', there are references and inferences to the circle of birth and death, and also to the thrush's defiant stand against the inevitable.

So, the poem, far from being totally bleak, is a demonstration of the arbitrary character of nature and fate. Even on a gloomy day, sublime things can happen. The 'Hope' that the poet refers to, and of which he says he is unaware, has echoes of the poet's own agnosticism wherein he has lost the power of belief in God.

He has not, however, lost his spirituality and there are echoes here of the Romantic movement and **pantheism**. We can detect in the poem references to Shelley's 'Ode to a Skylark' but the emphasis is very different. Although the singing is 'ecstatic', a word which

KEY TERM

Pantheism: The notion that God is everything and everywhere.

Shelley also uses, it does not move the poet/observer to joy but only to reflection. The poem reflects a reaction against the optimism and 'brightness' of Romanticism and thus inevitably draws different conclusions from Shelley.

✳✳✳✳SUMMARY ✳✳✳✳

The major themes of Hardy's work are:

- Working-class men struggling to better themselves through education.

- Family background and breeding.

- Sexuality.

- The role of women.

- Freedom of the individual from unthinking social oppression.

- The effects of industrialization and progress on individual lives.

- Landscape as metaphor and psychological setting for human drama.

- Ancient superstitions and their power over current lives.

- Deceit and hypocrisy.

- Fatalism and stoicism, sorrow, loss and regret.

Major Works: Later Novels

THE MAYOR OF CASTERBRIDGE

The Mayor of Casterbridge is in many ways different from Hardy's other novels. It is not a novel of courtship; there is no complex, sensual female character at its core and in terms of pure 'story' it is the fastest paced, most breathless of the novels. The novel is also seen as, in some respects at least, conforming to a classical form of tragedy in which a central hero is fated by the tragic flaws within his own character.

A novel of secrets and lies

The Mayor of Casterbridge would seem more than any other Hardy novel to be a novel that is built on secrets. The tragedy of the novel arises from the simple impossibility of such foundations. In this sense *The Mayor of Casterbridge* is a highly moral story with a very simple morality for it insists that whatever else, 'lying doesn't pay'. The terrible secret, that of the sale by Henchard of his wife to a sailor for five guineas while drunk, lies at the heart of the novel. It is the remorse following this incident which leads Henchard to renounce drink for the space of twenty years and it is the very public discovery of his shameful secret which speeds him from a position of power and prosperity into destitution and ultimately death. That point of turn in the novel is marked clearly and emphatically by Hardy:

> On that day – almost at that minute – he passed the ridge of prosperity and honour, and began to descend rapidly on the other side. It was strange how soon he sank in esteem.
>
> *The Mayor of Casterbridge*, Chapter 31

The novel seems to be full of untold tales, some arising from that central act of shame while others are spun for their own devious purpose. Having acquired a wife in such a strange fashion, the sailor Newson now has the problem of keeping her. His solution is to fabricate, to concoct a story that will convince her she is both morally and legally his. In this he succeeds, as Susan tells Henchard when they are reunited in Casterbridge:

> 'I thought I owed him faithfulness to the end of one of our lives – foolishly I believed there was something solemn and binding in the bargain; I thought that even in honour I dared not desert him when he had paid so much for me in good faith.'
>
> *The Mayor of Casterbridge*, Chapter 11

That Susan is depicted so frequently in terms of her limited intellect makes her acquiescence easy enough. Newson tells Henchard:

> 'As you in all likelihood know, she was simple-minded enough to think that the sale was in a way binding. She was as guiltless o' wrong-doing in that particular as a saint in the clouds.'
>
> *The Mayor of Casterbridge*, Chapter 41

Like all the lies in the novel, that of Newson's is destined finally to be uncovered. Her discovery, from one to whom she had confided, that his claim on her is 'a mockery' leads directly to another lie and also, of course, to another secret. To free Susan from her unhappiness, Newson constructs a report of his own death off the coast of Newfoundland. Susan now believes herself to be his widow and so is free to seek out Henchard. The arrival of Susan at Casterbridge and her resumed relations with Henchard necessitate further secrets – the need to hide from Casterbridge and even Elizabeth-Jane that Henchard and Susan are anything but distant relations before they re-marry. Into this is spun yet another secret – that of the two Elizabeth-Janes, different versions of which are believed at various times by Henchard, Susan and Elizabeth-Jane herself.

The second secret

If Henchard's secret leads to such a trail of deception, the second big secret in the novel fares little better. Lucetta's relationship with Henchard in Jersey is a part of her history which, if she is to retain/regain respectability in Casterbridge must be left behind. As readers we are introduced to the existence of Lucetta long before she arrives in person. Early in their friendship, Henchard chooses to tell Farfrae this part of his life story. Lucetta's appearance at Casterbridge is because, as she writes to Henchard, 'I ought to endeavour to disperse the shade which my étourderie flung over my name' (an 'étourderie' is a careless act or blunder). The étourderie refers to the liaison with Henchard many years before when he had supposed Susan dead and he had visited Jersey overrun by a bout of depression (this in itself can be seen as another act of deception arising directly from the wife sale).

The impossibility of keeping such secrets is indicated early in the story as Lucetta inadvertently lets slip to Elizabeth-Jane her true place of origin:

> 'Well for that matter, in my native isle speaking French does not go for much. It is rather the other way.'
> 'Where is your native isle?'
> It was with rather more reluctance that Miss Templeman said, 'Jersey'.
>
> *The Mayor of Casterbridge*, Chapter 22

What exactly went on between Henchard and Lucetta in Jersey is never revealed explicitly in the novel. The reader, who usually enjoys the full confidence of the narrator, is on this occasion kept at a distance. Henchard reveals one version of events to Farfrae:

> But being together in the same house, and her feeling warm, we got naturally intimate. I won't go into particulars of what our relations were. It is enough to say that we honestly meant to marry. There arose a scandal, which did me no harm, but was of course ruin to her.
>
> *The Mayor of Casterbridge*, Chapter 12

The suggestion here is that the relationship was intimate and sexual, after all Henchard tells, 'they meant to marry'. A second and very different version is revealed to the reader by Lucetta in a fiery conversation with Henchard:

'How can you speak so!' she answered, firing quickly. 'Knowing that my only crime was the indulging in a foolish girl's passion for you with too little regard for correctness, and that I was what I call innocent all the time they called me guilty, you ought not to be so cutting!'

The Mayor of Casterbridge, Chapter 25

The implication here is different. A 'foolish girl's passion' is very different from what is implied by Henchard's 'we got naturally intimate'. That Henchard tells they meant to marry while Lucetta refers to their relationship as 'innocent' pulls further veils over what may or may not have happened in Jersey. The letters which Lucetta wrote to Henchard are read by Jopp but are not in the public eye of the reader. The secret may also have been revealed by Lucetta on her deathbed to Farfrae, but again we are placed by Hardy outside this intimacy:

What, and how much, Farfrae's wife ultimately explained to him of her past entanglement with Henchard, when they were alone in the solitude of that sad night, cannot be told.

The Mayor of Casterbridge, Chapter 40

Other secrets in the text

Why, we have to ask, can it not be told? Possibly to protect Victorian sensibilities, or perhaps as a narrative device, heightening the possibility of animosity between Farfrae and Henchard? Whatever lies behind this secret it is only one of a large number of parts of the story which are never fully revealed to the reader. The most obvious gap in the narrative is that surrounding the eighteen years between the sale of Susan and her reappearance in Casterbridge. Some parts of this are filled in for us by Susan, Henchard and Newson but even so there is much that is not revealed:

* the death of the original Elizabeth-Jane

* the birth of the new Elizabeth-Jane

* the rise of Henchard to his position as leading businessman and mayor despite his headstrong nature, poor business practice, lack of

accounting skill and poor management of people all of which are central to his downfall.

Similarly, we are given little sense of Farfrae's history. Just why is it he has left, and never has any wish to return to Scotland, a place which he turns to in song with such great frequency?

As readers of *The Mayor of Casterbridge* we are often placed in an ambiguous position. We are privvy to much that is held secret by the narrative – we know of the sale of Susan, we know something of the secrets of Jersey, we know the truth of Elizabeth-Jane's origin – but at the same time other parts of the story are withheld from us.

The secrets which so permeate the narrative are also present in the very form of the novel. This technique of withholding and so engaging but never satisfying the reader's curiosity is one which Hardy develops in later novels.

Hardy was writing before Freud.

TESS OF THE D'URBERVILLES

A masterpiece?

This is perhaps Hardy's most **affective** novel, drawing us in, beguiling us with Tess's beauty, tempting us with Tess's sensuality and forcing us to confront our own morality as Hardy's 'President of the Immortals in Aeschlyean

> **KEY TERM**
>
> Affective: Having an emotion-influencing effect.

phrase' has his sport with Tess. It is certainly seen by many as his greatest work. As Robert Gittings puts it:

> *Tess of the d'Urbervilles* is his masterpiece, the fruit of over twenty years of a novelist's career, and of the chrysalis passion of a poet spreading new wings.
>
> Gittings, R., *The Older Hardy* (Penguin, 1978) p.98

Tess is the story of a young woman seduced or raped, (it is still the subject of considerable debate as to which it is) by an ersatz aristocrat. While the child from this sexual act dies early and sadly is buried unchristened, the consequences for Tess herself resound throughout the novel.

Of all the novels, *Tess* is the one that demands to be read more than once. The intensity of its tragedy, our enforced empathy for its **eponymous** heroine, the language of sensuality and seduction which pervade the novel all serve to dull if not dispel our critical judgement for certainly the first if not the second or third readings. That it is not until

> **KEY TERM**
>
> Eponymous Hero or heroine whose name appears in the title of the work e.g. *Don Juan*, *Robinson Crusoe*, *The Mayor of Casterbridge*.

perhaps the fourth (or even the eighth or ninth) reading we begin to question aspects of its construction is a testament to Hardy's creative genius. Lionel Johnson, in *The Art of Thomas Hardy* (1894), for example, commented: 'I read Tess eight or ten times with perfect enthusiasm- it is great literature – but finally, difficulties at first unfelt began to appear.'

A flawed masterpiece?

So just what is wrong with *Tess*? There are the usual gripes about Hardy's reliance upon coincidence and over-inflated language but also particular problems with the two men. Alec's sudden conversions from sinner to saint and back again are seen as problematic, as is Angel's unbearable hypocrisy.

One of the difficulties for readers of the novel would seem to be that while the roots of the story reside in Victorian **melodrama**, the novel itself vastly exceeds the restrictions of this form. In the conventional Victorian melodrama the poor but beautiful young maiden is preyed upon by the villainous aristocrat. His attempts at seduction are foiled by the dashing young man, who either kills or ruins the aristocrat. The hero then marries the heroine and they both live happily ever after. Of course in *Tess* it doesn't quite work that way. In Hardy's novel the whole story is subverted. Tess is seduced by the aristocrat and the hero not only fails to rescue her but also cruelly abandons her. The aristocrat is not even a real aristocrat and it is Tess herself who can trace a noble ancestry. Tess as a character does not always fit too comfortably into the role of vulnerable heroine. This is partly, as many critics have established, because it is her sensuality that defines her vulnerability and also that she at times shows a range of behaviours which seem to take her outside the role of helpless victim.

KEY TERM

Melodrama A play that was highly popular with Victorian audiences. It was characterized by sensationalism and the battle of good against evil. It had a powerful influence upon the popular Victorian novels as well as the work of serious novelists such as Hardy and Dickens.

Tess as a character

For many critics, then, it is within the character of Tess herself that the greatest problems arise. For critic Laura Claridge, the submissiveness and vulnerability which define Tess's character do not sit easily alongside her other traits such as cleverness, shrewdness and strength. While her submissiveness allows Hardy to explain her two sexual liaisons with Alec there are many occasions where she defies and even colludes with his expressions of affection and lust. There is, for example, the strawberry eating scene:

> Tess wished to abridge her visit as much as possible; but the young man was pressing, and she consented to accompany him. He conducted her about the lawns, and flower-beds, and conservatories; and thence to the fruit-garden and greenhouses, where he asked her if she liked strawberries.
>
> 'Yes,' said Tess, 'when they come.'
>
> 'They are already here.' D'Urberville began gathering specimens of the fruit for her, handing them back to her as he stooped; and, presently, selecting a specially fine product of the 'British Queen' variety, he stood up and held it by the stem to her mouth.
>
> 'No – no!' she said quickly, putting her fingers between his hand and her lips. 'I would rather take it in my own hand.'
>
> 'Nonsense!' he insisted; and in a slight distress she parted her lips and took it in.
>
> *Tess of the d'Urbervilles*, Chapter 5

Claridge comments that 'it is precisely because Tess chooses her sexual initiation – that she knows what she is about – that makes this scene highly erotic.' (Claridge L., 'Tess: A Less Than Pure Woman Ambivalently Presented' printed in Widdowson, P. op. cit, p. 69) That Tess continues to eat the offered strawberries, 'eating in a half-pleased, half-reluctant state whatever d'Urberville offered her,' suggests some of the ambivalence and, as Claridge points out anticipates her reaction to the seduction/rape which will soon follow.

One of the fascinating ambiguities of the novel lies in the degree to which Tess is portrayed as a sexualized woman. It is her sexuality which leads to her downfall and yet she is, Hardy insists in his subtitle, a 'pure' woman. She is seen by both Alec and Angel as a seductress and yet is also presented as a victim, seduced or raped, depending on your viewpoint, by the one, beguiled and then insensitively spurned by the other.

Of course, Hardy was not being wholly naïve in using the word 'pure', which to Victorians had strong associations with virginity and sexual fidelity. In using it he opens the possibility for other meanings, such as pure in heart or in spirit. He thus directly challenges prevailing sexual attitudes by suggesting that sexual experience outside marriage should not in itself condemn human beings. This is a theme explored much more deeply in *Jude*.

Visual impact of Tess

Part of the appeal of *Tess* is that it is an intensely sensuous novel, appealing to all of our senses but particularly the visual. This is what Peter Widdowson calls Hardy's proto-cinematic technique where the narration seems to describe scenes with cinematic clarity. The May-dance where Angel first sees Tess, the lush splendour of the Vale of Blackmoor, the contrast with the desolation of Flintcomb-Ash, the astonishing scene at Stonehenge or the last chapter where Angel and Liza-Lu watch the raising of the black flag from the top of the great West Hill are four examples of this technique.

The sensuality of the novel can be seen in this wonderfully evocative passage:

> The outskirt of the garden in which Tess found herself had been left uncultivated for some years, and was now damp and rank with juicy grass which sent up mists of pollen at a touch; and with tall blooming weeds emitting offensive smells – weeds whose red and yellow and purple hues formed a polychrome as dazzling as that of cultivated flowers. She went stealthily as a cat through this profusion of growth, gathering cuckoo-spittle on her skirts, cracking snails that were underfoot, staining her hands with thistle-milk and slug-slime, and rubbing off upon her naked arms sticky blights which, though snow-white on the apple-tree trunks, made madder stains on her skin; thus she drew quite near to Clare, still unobserved of him.
>
> *Tess of the d'Urbervilles*, Chapter 19

This passage is illustrative of Hardy's deep and complex use of both realism and **symbolism**. The scene is **synaesthetic** in that it heightens all our senses and alerts us to possible meanings and suggestions beyond the mere description itself. What is astonishing about this scene is its sheer fecundity, it is positively oozing with life and vitality. In walking through the uncultivated garden Tess is associated with this fecundity, and as she sweeps through she seems somehow to absorb the sticky fluids of nature. The language is unashamedly that of arousal. Tess abandons herself to the experience as she would to sensitive lovemaking. The reader is left to make those connections.

KEY TERMS

Symbolism: or more properly **symbolism** (with a small 's') is the use of one image or concept to represent another. In Hardy the weather is often used to symbolize mood. In the first chapter of *The Return of the Native* Hardy's complex descriptions of landscape and weather symbolize the psychological territory his characters will inhabit within the narrative.

Synaesthesia: In this context, a metaphor where an effect produced by stimulating all the senses suggests other states.

Landscape and emotion

In *Tess*, like so often in Hardy's novels, the landscape reflects the psychological threads of the novel and sets the emotional temperature. When Tess first arrives at the Vale of the Great Dairies, the scene before her is lush, productive and peaceful. It echoes her mood and her state of mind.

> Either the change in the quality of the air from heavy to light, or the sense of being amid new scenes where there were no invidious eyes upon her, sent up her spirits wonderfully. Her hopes mingled with the sunshine in an ideal photosphere which surrounded her as she bounded along against the soft south wind. She heard a pleasant voice in every breeze, and in every bird's note seemed to lurk a joy.
>
> *Tess of the d'Urbervilles*, Chapter 16

After she has been abandoned by Clare, we find her at Flintcomb Ash, picking turnips in a vast brown field, dwarfed by earth and sky. The place is barren and flinty, bereft of hope or joy and again parallels Tess's situation. And, of course, it is no accident that Tess is arrested at Stonehenge: historically a possible site of human sacrifice and a pagan symbol of the life–death cycle. As Angel Clare (and no less than sixteen policemen) watch the sleeping form of Tess until a shaft of light shines upon her and wakes her the symbolism is all too apparent. Here is Hardy's 'pure woman', a virgin in all but actuality, lying on the sacrificial slab, a point confirmed by her final words in the novel, 'I am ready'.

JUDE THE OBSCURE

Autobiographical links

Jude was Hardy's last novel. Despite Hardy's own denials, the story has strong and obvious autobiographical elements. For example, there is the simple man unable to gain a university place because of poverty and lack of influence – a man involved in the building/architectural trade.

Ambivalence

> 'I think I should begin to be afraid of you, Jude, the moment you had contracted to cherish me under a Government stamp, and I was licensed to be loved on the premises by you – Ugh, how horrible and sordid! Although, as you are, free, I trust you more than any other man in the world.'
>
> *Jude the Obscure*, Part 5, Chapter 1

The comments of Sue Bridehead as she and Jude debate marriage sum up much of the style and spirit of the novel. It demonstrates the ambivalence which so characterizes the relationship of Sue and Jude. Ambivalence is a hallmark of *Jude* as we shall see later. Sue's comments also forcefully demonstrate Hardy's propensity to shock. The phrases 'licensed to be loved on the premises' and 'under a Government stamp', are a chilling description of marriage, especially as it existed for Victorian women. Such views might not seem shocking today but they would have been anathema to Hardy's readership in 1891.

Themes in *Jude*

Centrally, the book is about oppression. Sue is oppressed by social mores about sexuality and a woman's role in society; Jude is oppressed by bourgeois middle-class educational thinking.

The major themes are threefold: the closed world of the middle-class educational elite and their tight grip on university education; the roles of women in a strongly patriarchal society and the desire of women to seek alternative modes of existence; the prevailing moral view that marriage and its sanctity is the only choice for decent people and, linked with this, the role of the church in maintaining dogma and social attitudes in a world where many were beginning to lose their faith.

Jude aspires to a university education at Christminster. Before he can begin to follow this ambition he is seduced by Arabella Donn and she tricks him into marrying her pretending she is pregnant. Marriage is Jude's only honourable course. The relationship is portrayed as being base and crude, with the protagonists unsuited to each other. The marriage disintegrates once carnality has waned and the pair separate, Arabella for Australia, Jude for Christminster.

In contrast, the relationship between Sue and Jude is largely spiritual. They feel like soul mates and find it hard to live apart. When Sue eventually allows intimacy and sexual union, things start to go wrong. Hardy shows Jude as struggling with his earthly desires of lust and drink, while Sue seems to exist in a state of continual vacillation between a perplexing and contradictory range of emotions, desires and moralities.

Hardy is at pains to depict his two central characters as being caught between several unassailable dichotomies. Jude is shown to struggle between the desire for spiritual and intellectual enlightenment and a darker baser desire for carnality. It is his sexual desire for the earthy Arabella which turns him from his early ambition towards academia and it is the impassioned kiss with Sue which turns him away from the Church. This kiss we are told, 'was a turning point in Jude's career'. While on the one hand he sees it as 'the purest moment of his faithful life', on the other hand this 'unlicensed tenderness' is felt by Jude to be incompatible with a religious calling 'in which sexual love was regarded as at its best a frailty, and at its worst damnation.' It is this conflict in Jude between the spiritual and the carnal which Hardy uses as the spit upon which Jude is slowly roasted. That this dilemma is so effective in bringing about Jude's downfall is hastened by his own sense of shame:

> I have the germs of every human infirmity in me, I verily believe – that was why I saw it was so preposterous of me to think of being a curate. I have cured myself of drunkenness I think; but I never know in what new form a suppressed vice will break out in me!
>
> *Jude the Obscure*, Part 5, Chapter 2

As Hardy points out in his preface to the first edition this is intended as a 'deadly war waged between spirit and flesh'.

Sue's dilemma would seem to be no less impossible: the wish to be loved and desired is linked with what we would now see as a neurotic level of sexual frigidity. There is also a most conscious portrayal of Sue as elusive, contrary, perverse: it seems that whatever aspect of Sue is presented to us in one moment will surely be contradicted by her the next. She, too, is depicted as a character at war with herself, never quite knowable either by Jude within the narrative nor by us as readers of Hardy's text.

Part of this enigmatic aspect of Sue is created by keeping us one step away from our own voyeuristic interest in the relationship of Jude and Sue. Hardy seems often to tease us. Has their relationship been consummated? Have they actually got married? The false trails planted by Hardy to mislead us on these points are interesting paths to follow.

The latter part of the book is dominated by the arrival of the lugubrious Father Time, a child whose moroseness hovers like Fate itself, and whose ultimate action in killing himself and the other children demonstrates the cruel caprices of life. Father Time comes to haunt Jude for his past mistakes and, like the incubus in 'The Withered Arm', ultimately exerts a strong malicious influence.

The letter killeth

Hardy's epigraph to the book was 'the letter killeth'. The writing and reading of letters, both literally as in the performing of writing, and less literally as in posted letters, would seem to play a central role in shaping the narrative.

Jude at one time aspires to be an intellectual man of letters and is cruelly unsuccessful in that endeavour. As a young man he naïvely imagines that in order to learn Greek he only has to read and transmute the words. His disappointment in discovering that he will have to learn a whole new code foreshadows the degree of effort he will have to put into attaining entry to university and the promise of intellectual attainment and middle class-status that he craves. Ironically also, it is a letter from the Master of Biblioll College that dashes Jude's hopes of such scholarship in a heartless and patronizing way. Letters feature in other ways too: Father Time leaves his parents a letter of explanation for the children's deaths, thus 'killing' Jude and Sue's relationship. As a final touch of irony, Jude is a man of letters in another sense: he carves words on plaques and headstones.

However, Hardy's main allusion in referring to the 'letter killeth' is to the 'letter' of Church and legal procedures – that setting in stone of love, that Government stamp and licence to be loved on the premises which eventually stifles Sue and Jude. Hardy was not expressing anything new here, but was capitalizing on a new wave of thought which was finding expression in **New Woman fiction**.

Hardy took this trend and developed the theme further, turning it to tragic proportions. In *Jude* he explores the consequences of prevailing social mores on individuals, and explores legalistic and 'natural' marriages without drawing any obvious conclusions. He was careful to deny that he was attacking marriage laws, but went on to say in the 1912 postscript to the book, that 'civil law should only be the enunciation of the law of nature.' The woolliness of this remark demonstrates confusions which probably beset many as they struggled to equate freedom with social and Church law.

> **KEY TERM**
>
> New Woman fiction: The New Woman movement of the 1890s sought individual and social freedoms for women, including: a rejection of marriage; a more honest approach to female sexuality; and a demand for more economic and personal independence. New Woman fiction explored some of these issues, some books becoming bestsellers, most notably Sarah Grand's *The Heavenly Twins*, George Egerton's *Keynotes*, and Grant Allen's *The Woman Who Did*. The movement was eclipsed by the suffragists who sought equality through the ballot box, rather than through personal and sexual freedom.

The story itself contains many contradictions, comparing as it does the failed marriages of Sue and Jude with the 'natural' marriage of the couple. Here, the alternative offered is not promiscuous (and loveless) sex, but a monogamous state remarkably like marriage. And yet Sue describes living in intimacy with Phillotson, her husband, while wishing to be in a union with Jude, as 'adultery, in any circumstances'. Further ambiguity is supplied by Jude's own behaviour:

> Although he is a victim of legalistic marriage and speaks violently against it, he behaves finally … as the law told a nineteenth century

husband he might do: he enforces his 'conjugal rights', not by force but by blackmail. Having agreed to live celibately with Sue he uses Arabella's return to force her into sexual relations.

Patricia Ingham, Introduction to World's Classics *Jude the Obscure*,
(Oxford, 1985)

Controversy

The book proved difficult for Hardy's contemporary readership to accept. It trampled over so many taboos at once. There were the graphically shocking images such as the pig's pizzle being thrown at Jude, the amateurish slaughter of a pig, and at least two gory porcine dismemberments. There was Hardy's attack on the insularity and elitism of the academic establishment. There were the unpleasant and graphic child murders and suicide. There was the unsettling search by women for new ways of existing with (or without) men, and the unconventional marital and carnal relationships of Jude, Arabella, Sue and Phillotson. Even the Church came off badly, being the source of quick atonement for Arabella, but condemning Sue to a largely unhappy and, eventually, barren life of servitude to Phillotson. Finally, there was the starkly bleak ending, with the hero Jude wasting away, his aspirations dashed.

The book remains stimulating to the modern reader because it offers no clear answers. There is a lack of conventional sympathetic hero/heroine and this makes the act of moral judgement difficult. It is not easy to say who is 'right' or 'wrong', and who is to blame when things go wrong. We are left to observe the unfolding tragedy in a state of half-suspended shock, particularly after the brutal hanging of the children 'DONE BECAUSE WE ARE TOO MENNY'. When Jude's health begins to fail at the end of the novel, it is described at too much of a distance, and in too little detail for us to become involved and sympathetic. We merely observe. Hardy, in his preface to the first edition, describes the tale as a 'series of seemings' with questions of 'their consistency, or their discordance, their permanence or their transitoriness, being regarded as not of the first moment.' Thus Hardy seems very modern to us because that is how literature works today.

✳✳✳✳SUMMARY ✳✳✳✳

- *The Mayor of Casterbridge* is a novel built upon secrets.

- This technique is used to withhold information from the reader, much of which is never revealed.

- *Tess of the d'Urbervilles* is usually seen as Hardy's masterpiece.

- It is also seen as a flawed masterpiece particularly in the presentation of its central character.

- *Jude the Obscure* explores four major themes: the elitism of the higher educational system; the role of women and their sexuality; marriage and its limitations; and the role of the Church in people's personal lives.

The President of the Immortals has his sport with Tess.

Major Works: The Poetry

VAST OUTPUT

It is not until you see a copy of Hardy's collected works that you become aware of the enormity of his output. There are nearly a thousand poems packed into 907 pages in the Wordsworth Poetry Library edition. They are poems which span the whole of his writing life though many were not written until after the publication of *Jude*.

Hardy obviously enjoyed writing poetry. He felt he was finally doing what he did best. In a famous comment of 1937 about the *Collected Poems*, Ezra Pound agreed with him: 'Now *there* is clarity. There *is* the harvest of having written twenty novels first' (quoted in David Wright's introduction to the Penguin *Thomas Hardy Selected Poetry*).

A CENTRAL CORE OF 'GOOD' POEMS

Given such a vast canon, this *Beginner's Guide* can only hope to point you in the right direction. You must discover for yourself, as have thousands before you, the beguiling quality and clear vision contained within Hardy's poetry. Critics and commentators often have a hard time trying to decide the worth of his poetry. One view remains that there is a core of his poems which is significant, with the rest serving only to produce diamonds out of coal. However, there is no coherent consensus as to what constitutes this worthy core, although many poems, such as 'The Darkling Thrush', occur fairly commonly when Hardy's poetry is discussed. What is clear is that Hardy is becoming more respected academically as a poet as the rising tide of new work about him shows.

Hardy was not a mannered or over-refined poet, except when he forgot himself and tried to show off, or when he became too self-conscious, as we notice at times in his prose writing. We have already seen in 'The

Darkling Thrush' (see Chapter 6), that his poetry can be beautiful, lucid and thoughtful. If we avoid the common tendency to see him merely as a lugubrious pessimist, there is much of value to be found.

Although you will undoubtedly wish to concentrate upon some of the core poems, you will also find great delight in picking out poems at random from the collected works. There are many more diamonds to be had than the critics would have you believe. Certainly one can see the 'harvest' to which Pound refers. The poems are a rich distillation of Hardy's major preoccupations. Often, the full flavour of any poem is not apparent until it has been read in sequence with other poems.

CONTROVERSY AND TABOO

Hardy's territory was firmly based in love and relationships and sex, time, place and death. An early poem, 'A Trampwoman's Tragedy', contains the seeds of many of his other poems and displays his tendency to grasp taboo subjects without fear.

It is based around the **ballad** format, telling the story of a woman driving her lover to kill his friend through jealousy. There is a strong sense of rhythm and the second line repeats the first in traditional style.

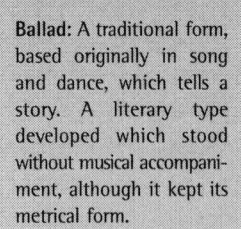

KEY TERM

Ballad: A traditional form, based originally in song and dance, which tells a story. A literary type developed which stood without musical accompaniment, although it kept its metrical form.

The poem explores familiar territory, the fickleness and instability of love together with the intensity of the feelings it provokes. Unlike most ballads, which are content with telling a narrative – often with moral overtones – as a way of fixing stories in collective consciousness, Hardy goes much further. There are unexplained things in the poem, most notably the motivation of the trampwoman. We are interested at a psychological level as to her motivation and why she goes to such dangerous limits to lie to her lover. We are left wondering why she decided to make him jealous in the first place and why she compounds the lie by wounding him with the falsehood that the baby she is carrying is not his. Thus, early in his writing career, Hardy has begun to explore relationships and 'immoral' behaviour. Many of Hardy's perpetual themes can be seen here: the unreliability of love; guilt; remorse; unexpected death; the gallows; the capriciousness of life. Indeed, the poem shocked his readers and was banned from school anthologies for many years. Despite this, the poem is accessible and enjoyable.

SIMPLICITY OF STYLE

The simple poem 'The Oxen', written much later, has become part of English culture. It is often still recited during Christmas festivities and is much loved. The first two verses read:

The Oxen

Christmas Eve, and twelve of the clock.
'Now they are all on their knees,'
An elder said as we sat in a flock
By the embers in hearthside ease.

We pictured the meek mild creatures where
They dwelt in their strawy pen,
Nor did it occur to one of us there
To doubt they were kneeling then.

This was written in 1915, three years after the death of Emma, and during probably the most bloody war ever witnessed by humankind. Although he wrote many poems on the evils of war, here he found time and poetic vision to write in a different vein. At first the poem seems childlike with its Sunday school pictures and naïve rural superstition that the animal kingdom all bowed down on Christmas Eve to honour the new-born Saviour, Jesus Christ.

It is the simplicity of the piece which gives it charm. The rhythm has a spring in its step and demonstrates something that Hardy was always seeking to achieve: an elegant variation in rhythm to avoid tedium. By using agricultural imagery ('strawy', 'barton') Hardy seems to be very consciously constructing a sense of rural simplicity. He creates a link between the narrative voice (the 'I' in the poem), the group of which he is a member (the 'we' of the poem), and the land of the narrator's childhood (the 'back then' in the poem). There is also a link with even further 'back then', the nativity and the animals in the stable in Bethlehem. It is also a Christian poem. Hardy's Christianity had waned by now, but in recollecting scenes from childhood a sense of it often returns.

HARDY AS THE POET OF LOSS AND LONGING

Beneath the surface of childhood fairy tale and naïve belief lies a deeper feeling of regret for that lost childhood, and for the loss of faith. The tone is wistful and reflective rather than sombre and depressing. Hardy talked of his poems being 'unadjusted impressions' and saw himself as much as a poet of record as anything else. His poems work at a microscopic level, offering varying and subtly different views of a life that changes unpredictably and according to chance.

Just as in the novels, the poems are all part of the same 'family' although clear distinctions can be observed between them. This is nowhere clearer than in the *Poems of 1912–13*. Hardy's marriage to Emma had not been very happy or successful in its later years.

Emma died in November 1912 and this sent Hardy into deep shock. Guilt and remorse triggered a torrent of poems about their early love, which these celebrate and reflect upon the first years of their relationship. It was a Hardy trait that he would dwell on past and pleasurable trysts, enjoying and heightening his experience of them. For example, the poems 'A Thunderstorm in Town', 'At an Inn', and 'Broken Appointment' are believed to be about his close but unconsummated affair with Mrs Arthur Henniker which began in 1893. He also wrote 'Thoughts of Phena' about Tryphena Sparks, his early love, after her death in 1893.

Hardy was a master love poet, able to explore love and marriage in such a depth that few can equal him. The *Poems of 1912–13* demonstrate this perfectly, and in particular the sequence of poems headed *Veteris vestigia flammae* ('ashes of an old fire'). These are probably the most studied of Hardy's poetry and they are a remarkably lucid and accessible body of work.

The *Poems of 1912–13* are concerned with the young Hardy's courtship of Emma Gifford before their marriage. Hardy had met her as he visited St Juliot to survey a church for restoration work, and they took many walks and rides along the Cornish cliffs, most notably Beeny Cliff, the 'Cliff with No Name' of *A Pair of Blue Eyes*. A look at 'The Walk' gives us a flavour.

> **The Walk**
> You did not walk with me
> Of late to the hill-top tree
>   By the gated ways.
>   As in earlier days;

> You were weak and lame,
>   So you never came.
> And I went alone, and I did not mind,
> Not thinking of you as left behind.
>
> I walked up there today
> Just in the former way;
>   Surveyed around
>   The familiar ground
>   By myself again:
>   What difference, then?
> Only that underlying sense
> Of the look of a room on returning thence.

Here, we have a poem with a piece missing – a verse not there. Where is the verse in the middle of the poem representing the middle and late years of what became a very unhappy marriage. It is this gap in the narrative which makes the poem more poignant and heightens the sense of loss.

The 'hill-top tree', which obviously once had romantic connotations, stands as a reminder of the loneliness of the writer. The reference to 'not thinking of you as left behind' is repeated in other poems, often in the sense that, in death, *she* has left *him*. We cannot, though, escape Hardy's irony in not minding leaving Emma behind on a walk when she was ill, when that is what seems to have happened in the marriage itself.

Another poem in the sequence, 'Rain on a Grave' has the poet viewing the grave of his departed wife in heavy rain. The rain at one level obviously represents the tears of remorse, these are the 'arrows of rain'. The dead lover hated the touch of rain on her skin yet now lies helpless under the onslaught: 'Clouds spout upon her/ Their waters amain/ In ruthless disdain'. There is a hint here that the deceased did not like the touch of her lover either, echoing Sue Bridehead in *Jude*, and suggesting one of the things that went wrong with Hardy's marriage.

In the third stanza the writer expresses the wish that their roles were reversed and that he should be the one to lay where she does now, or better, 'together were folded away there/ Exposed to one weather we both'. The last verse appears to mark a coming to terms with the death, describing her using images of daisies 'like stars on the ground/ Till she form part of them', and leaving her 'Loved beyond measure'.

ELEGY OR ANTI-ELEGY?

The love poems both to Emma and others are in the elegiac tradition. However, modern criticism is beginning to see beyond the mere celebration of people after they have died. In an essay entitled 'The Modernity of Thomas Hardy's Poetry', J.P. Riquelme points to Hardy as writing 'anti-elegiac **elegies**' (Kramer, D, *The Cambridge Companion to Thomas Hardy*, (UP)).

> **KEY TERM**
>
> Elegy: A poem of mourning in reflective mode, as in Thomas Grays's 'Elegy Written in a Country Churchyard'; Alfred Lord Tennyson's 'In Memoriam'; and G.M. Hopkins's 'The Wreck of the Deutschland'.

With reference to 'Rain on a Grave', Riquelme detects not only the conventional elements of the life and death cycle, and reconciliation through tears, but also a strong sexual undercurrent which was not present in the traditional elegiac form. He points to the erotic connotations of 'arrows of rain' and the penetrating effect on her body, and to the green blades of grass which will soon be growing 'from her mound' (her pubic mound). From this he concludes that Hardy was being subversive, using an untraditional violence of imagery and expressing the view that the earth can possess her whereas he cannot (and could not).

The *Veteris vestigia flammae* sequence is full of imagery. Cliffs and the sea pervade all the poems. Then there is: the hill-top tree ('The Walk'); cloud imagery and the association with tears ('Rain on A Grave'); daisies showing like stars on Emma's grave (also 'Rain on A Grave'); hurricanes, high seas and a shipwreck ('I Found Her Out There'). The images serve to set the love story in context and, as in all of Hardy's work, allow the emotional values to be enhanced and transformed. They set Hardy as one of the last of the great provincial poets, in the mould of the Romantic poet John Clare, but also as a writer with strong connections with the Modernist movement.

THE WORLD AS A 'WELTER OF FUTILE UNDOING'

One poem that shows this connection is 'In Tenebris'. Its interest lies in that it was written between 1895 and 1896, just at the time when Hardy was in the depth of despair after the reaction to *Jude*.

The poem is in three parts, each different in metrical style. Part 1 uses the imagery of winter to set the mood. We are in 'the lone frosts black-length', where 'leaves flee to dun', and 'flower petals flee'. The tone is black and talks of 'bereavement pain', 'his heart who no heart hath', and one who 'waits in unhope'. The subject is death but in this case, no one has died. Perhaps the death is of Hardy as a writer of prose. It seems as if Hardy is waiting and wishing for death. As a study in depression, Part I has few equals.

Part II is much more expansive with longer line lengths. In it, Hardy berates 'the stout upstanders', the critics who smugly feel 'all's well with us', and who 'breezily go they, breezily come' as 'their dust smokes around their career.' There is more spirit in this section although the writer feels he is 'one born out of due time, who has no calling here'.

Part III returns to the theme of death but in a more reflective light. The images are of spring/summer with the poet remembering how he 'fashioned and furbished the earth into a summer-seeming order', and where he was in a state of innocence 'ere I had learnt that the world was a welter of futile doing.' He mentions a 'she', someone who upheld him and whom he deemed 'matchless'. The poem ends with the sentiment that it might have been better to have died before he gained worldly knowledge. A mixture of critical rejection and marital despair seems to have driven him to chart the length of his depression without feeling it necessary to supply a positive ending. In his poetry, Hardy could be in total control and was no longer under the dead hand of the over-censorious publisher as he was with his fiction.

HARDY THE POET OF WAR

Hardy is a modern poet in the sense that war became one of his main themes. Although most of his war poetry was written before 1914, it carries a strong sense of futility. Hardy had been fascinated by Napoleon and his great epic 'The Dynasts' examines the Napoleonic Wars in some detail. Later came the Boer War, one of the first great modern wars of mass destruction, from which Hardy drew much inspiration. The Boer War provided material for eleven of the 'War Poems' which appeared in *Poems of the Past and Present* in 1902. The most well known of these is 'Drummer Hodge', a scathingly ironical piece which attacks the whole notion of Britain's imperialist aspirations by using as its central character working-class anti-hero, Drummer Hodge, a character who would not be out of place in the colonial India of Rudyard Kipling.

The callous horror of war is made clear in the first two lines: 'They throw in Drummer Hodge, the rest/ Uncoffined, just as found'. The use of the word 'throw' emphasizes the violence of the act and its lack of respect. It hints at untold bodies buried anonymously in this way. The use of his name heightens the sense of anonymity as the corpse is dumped in the mass grave. Hodge was a name often used to describe an everyman country figure – a labourer – and thus ties the soldier to the rural working class. The notion of Drummer Hodge being a son of the soil ironically accentuates his burial – his return to the soil.

Seventeen more war poems were published in *Moments of Vision and Miscellaneous Verses* in 1917. One striking poem from this collection is 'The Men Who March Away', written in 1914. It demonstrates Hardy's ability to present a seemingly simple poem which then reveals complex subtleties.

An example of this in the poem is the triple viewpoint presented: those of the soldiers themselves, the omniscient writer and the impotent, voyeuristic reader. The poem is ostensibly a 'Song of the Soldiers', and gives a fairly conventional view of soldiers singing and marching off to battle in the belief that 'Victory crowns the just'. However, the writer injects an irony into the piece so that we are aware of both the sentiments of the men singing themselves to war and of the terrible fate that will befall their innocence. Thus the poet shows his colours. The soldiers' song addresses a third party, the reader, who can only look on in dumb disbelief. 'Men who march away' is a reflection of the stirring patriotic songs used at the time to bolster resolve, and when repeated as the last line, becomes a chilling prediction that they are marching away forever. Hardy does not talk about 'our boys', he uses the word 'men' to describe the youngsters marching away, for men they really are and as men (and thus husbands, lovers, fathers and brothers) they will die.

CHANGING SENSIBILITIES

Hardy's poetic journey into the twentieth century was marked by a growing awareness of a new order in literature – the rise of Modernism. Although not a Modernist himself, his later work begins to foreshadow and echo the new sensibilities. In 'He Resolves to Say No More', one of his last poems, we can get a flavour of the change. In the poem, as the title suggests, the poet vows to silence himself: to spare the world from any more 'ails' so that 'What I have learnt no man shall know.'

In a marked reversal of traditional artistic temperament, the poet decides to be silent – a contradiction in terms. If there is to be silence, then others must fill it with their own noise. By choosing silence the poet also chooses to leave things unresolved, for although he professes to have learned a great deal, 'What I have learnt no man shall know.'

This leaves us with an impression of a silent scream, or a man going to his death but still figuratively alive in his coffin. The silence becomes a motif in such writers as Samuel Beckett where what is not said means much more than what is uttered. The 'charnel-eyed Pale Horse' carries with it nightmare qualities so familiar to the modern reader. Leaving things unfinished, or rather accepting that things cannot always be resolved comfortably in life, is a familiar idea to Modernists, and the fractured nature of existence that this implies is very much a view in keeping with its time and with the rest of twentieth-century literature. Beckett's play *Waiting for Godot* consists of numerous silences which we now understand to say as much as the words. This is a technique which became the main characteristic of playwrights such as Harold Pinter.

In another late poem, 'We are Getting to the End', the starkness characteristic of some later writers is very clear:

> We know that even as larks in cages sing
> Unthoughtful of deliverance from the curse
> That holds them lifelong in a latticed hearse,
> We ply spasmodically for our pleasuring.

There is a deep self-absorption here, along with a bleakness of vision and sense of hopeless despair which can be seen as a motif of the twentieth century. If nothing else his dark themes and ways of tackling difficult subjects opened the doors for the Modernists to walk through.

Hardy's Wessex – modern style

✳✳✳✳SUMMARY ✳✳✳✳

- Hardy saw himself as a poet first and a novelist second.

- He felt that his poems could express better the themes of his novels.

- His output covers a period spanning the Napoleonic Wars to the First World War, and foreshadows the Second World War.

- His poetry came to reflect Modernist ideas.

- Hardy's poetry:

  - is becoming more respected in academic circles

  - spans the whole period of his writing career

  - is multifaceted

  - is more complex than it often first appears

  - uses many different poetic styles

  - changes slowly over time.

Critical Approaches to Hardy

FLAVOUR OF CONTEMPORARY CRITICISM

> Few people will deny the terrible dreariness of this tale, which, except during the few hours spent with cows, has not a gleam of sunshine anywhere.
>
> review of Tess in Saturday Review 16 January 1893, reprinted in Cox, R.G. (ed.) Thomas Hardy: The Critical Heritage (Routledge & Kegan Paul) p.190

Hardy's highly sensitive nature was frequently bruised by the adverse comments of his contemporaries, particularly by the furore following the publication of his two most controversial novels, *Tess* and *Jude*.

While the majority of critics viewed *Tess* in a very positive light there were others who objected to both its morality and its pessimism (or 'Tessimism' as some critics expressed it). Mowbray Morris in the *Quarterly Review* (April 1892) complained of Hardy that he had 'gratuitously chosen to tell a coarse and disagreeable story in a coarse and disagreeable manner. (ibid. p.220) Another critic wrote:

> Hardy postulates an all powerful being endowed with the baser human passions, who turns everything to evil and rejoices in the mischief he has wrought.
>
> Cited in Hardy, F., The Life of Thomas Hardy, (1930), Book 2, p.4

What made *Tess* so controversial was not the plot of an innocent girl defiled, which had been portrayed in many other novels of the period but rather the polemical tone of the work. Boumelha identifies four aspects of the work which scandalized late Victorian sensibilities:

* the discussion in public and literature of sex roles and of the double standard;

* the ambivalence of Tess's feelings for her child;

* Tess's concealment of her past from Angel;

* the second 'fall' where Tess seemingly willingly submits to becoming Alec's mistress.

If reviews of *Tess* had been uneven, it was the publication of *Jude* that caused a storm of hostile critical reactions, the force of which both surprised and disturbed Hardy. The burning of a copy of *Jude* by Bishop How was disturbing enough but what hurt him the most was the hostile comments from friends such as Edmund Gosse who told him that *Jude* was the most indecent novel he had ever written. Gosse's review in the *St James' Gazette* had been somewhat more supportive but still pronounced: 'We rise from the perusal of it stunned with a sense of the hollowness of existence' (Millgate op. cit. p.370). Hardy wrote in the 1912 postscript to *Jude* that the effect of the experience had been that of 'completely curing me of further interest in novel writing', an effect much disputed by recent biographers, who suggest there was far more in Hardy's decision than anger at his critics.

HARDY AND THE MODERNISTS

Hardy's novels, despite the controversy which surrounded their publication, are seen to belong to a Victorian tradition. The poetry which began to be published from 1898 onwards is more difficult to place. The rise of Hardy's popularity as a poet is mirrored by a huge shift in the writing of literature and its appreciation: that of Modernism. Perhaps part of the reason why the poetry has been so often over-looked lies in its incongruity with the period of its publication. It has been too often associated

> **KEY TERM**
>
> Georgian poetry: A term now used pejoratively to refer to the worst of poetry written in the early part of the last century. Such poetry is much criticized for its pastoral and escapist style.

with the now largely forgotten, **Georgian poetry** of the early twentieth century.

The Modernists themselves felt Hardy's poetry was out of kilter with the radically new styles and forms they were adopting. Nevertheless, as we have seen, the themes of his later work anticipate the Modernist movement.

In some ways Hardy stood for much of what the Modernists consciously rejected. A comparison between Hardy's *Moments of Vision* published in 1917 and T.S. Eliot's *Prufrock and Other Observations* published in the same year shows how great the distance is between Hardy's work and that of the Modernists in terms of form and style, although not necessarily in terms of theme and mood. Eliot was at one stage highly critical of Hardy, commenting:

> He was indifferent even to the precepts of good writing: he wrote sometimes overpoweringly well, but always very carelessly: at times his style touches sublimity without ever having passed through the stage of being good.
>
> T.S. Eliot, *After Strange Gods* (Faber and Faber, 1934) p.55

Yet to argue this is to be over-simplistic. The Modernists themselves were perhaps too close to Hardy to see the parallels and to acknowledge his radicalism and his contribution to their movement.

LEAVIS AND THE NEW CRITICS

The influence of F.R. Leavis as decider of taste in the middle of the last century was profound even if his tastes now seem highly conservative and his tone dictatorial and elitist. 'The great English novelists are Jane Austen, George Eliot, Henry James and Joseph Conrad' he declared on page 1 of *The Great Tradition* (Penguin, 1948). Hardy is dismissed with a quote from Henry James:

> The good little Thomas Hardy has scored a great success with *Tess of the d'Urbervilles*, which is chock-full of faults and falsity, and yet has a singular charm.
>
> (p.34)

Leavis conceded that *Jude* was impressive although found that it hadn't the 'rightness with which the great novelists show their profound sureness of their essential purpose'. (op. cit. p.34) The poetry had been similarly dismissed by the great man in his earlier judgement *New Bearings in English Poetry* with the comment that Hardy was 'a naïve poet of simple attitudes and outlook' (Penguin, 1932, p.52).

RAYMOND WILLIAMS AND THE ENGLISH NOVEL

If Leavis was dismissive, Williams was most certainly not. His work was influential in the process of placing Hardy back into the English **canon**:

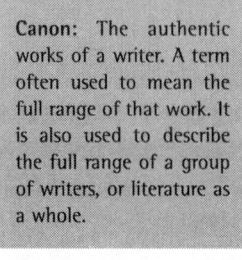

KEY TERM

Canon: The authentic works of a writer. A term often used to mean the full range of that work. It is also used to describe the full range of a group of writers, or literature as a whole.

> The more I read Hardy the surer I am that he is a major novelist, but also that the problem of describing his work is central to the problem of understanding the whole development of the English novel.

> Williams, R., *The English Novel from Dickens to Lawrence*
> (Paladin, 1974) p.79

Williams saw Hardy's novels as exploring the tension between different worlds: custom and education, work and ideas, the old and the new. He sees Hardy as a writer who explores the conflicts which are central to the process of change and as a writer who situated himself in the abyss between the position of educated observer and passionate participant. Williams also brings to Hardy criticism a focus on social class and explores Hardy's concern with the restrictions imposed by class as explored within almost all the novels but particularly *Jude* and *Return of the Native*.

WANTED: A GOOD HARDY CRITIC

In an essay with this title written in 1966, the poet Philip Larkin laments the absence of good critics of both Hardy's poetry and his prose. He speculates that perhaps the writing is too simple to require elucidation or that it is just that a good critic has yet to materialize. Larkin sees the suffering that lies at the heart of much of Hardy's writing and takes issue with critics who try to deny the sadness inherent in it. He sees this sadness as a sign of Hardy's maturity, associating the suffering depicted in his work with a sensitivity to its causes. For Larkin there is nothing mechanical or fatalistic about the suffering but rather:

> ... the continual imaginative celebration of what is both the truest and most important element in life, most important in the sense of most necessary to spiritual development. To examine this element, his perception of it and treatment in literary terms would be the business of the proper study of Hardy which, as far as I know, has yet to be written.
>
> Larkin, P., *Required Writing: Miscellaneous Pieces* 1955–82
>
> (Faber and Faber, 1983, pp.172–3)

THE SHIFT

The lamentable absence of good criticism has been matched by a curious ambivalence among academics regarding Hardy's significance and status as a great novelist. Readers, in contrast, have continued to buy and read his books with what seems an undiluted enthusiasm. Indeed this gap between critical acclaim and popular acclaim continued until near the end of the twentieth century. Early criticism dwelt on problems of morality: that subjects such as seduction, sexual relations outside marriage, illegitimacy, suicide, atheism should not be fictionalized, particularly where the novelist himself proclaims such unconventional views. Later criticism focused on three problems:

* the sheer unrelieved pessimism of the stories;

* the reliance upon coincidence as a structural device within the plot;

* the use of language, often seen as heavy-handed and over-burdened with allusion.

Since this time there has been a shift in literary criticism in general and in Hardy criticism in particular. This has been largely a change in methodology, notably the development of what is now referred to as **theory**. The development of theory has brought with it an interest in the way in which we, as readers, as students, as critics, read literary texts. One notable shift is seen in the interest in the form, that is the way in which the novels are both structured and written.

Before looking at some modern approaches to Hardy it must be added that the field of Hardy criticism is one which is not much used as a

KEY TERM

Theory: Something of a 'catch all' term which is applied to the wave-like succession of new approaches to literature beginning in the 1970s. The term 'literary theory' is frequently used, but 'theory' captures the multi-disciplinary nature of these movements.

testing ground for new ideas. There has been in the last few years a variety of new approaches to his work but this interest does tend to lag behind that applied to other nineteenth-century writers such as Dickens and Eliot. The recent publication of collections of modern critical essays about Hardy's work is an encouraging sign.

HARDY AND REALISM

The traditional view of Hardy has been to see him as a realist writer whose half dozen really great novels, and similar number of minor (and somewhat flawed) novels, are enough on their own to place him in the canon of literature. Yet Widdowson among many others today questions this simple categorization of Hardy as a writer of social realism. He comments that Hardy had a consciously held contradictory relationship with Realism as an art form. He cites Hardy writing in *The Life*:

> Art is a disproportioning – (i.e., distorting throwing out of proportion) – of realities, to show more clearly the features that matter in those realities, which, if merely copied or reported inventorially, might possibly be observed but would more probably be overlooked. Hence 'realism' is not art.
>
> Widdowson, P. op. cit. p.14

FEMINIST APPROACHES TO HARDY

Kirsten Brady suggests that examining the changing responses to Hardy's construction of gender from 1871 to the present is a way of tracing the broader picture, that is the way in which sexuality has been constructed in Britain and the USA in the same period. In the nineteenth and early twentieth century Hardy's women were seen as 'organisms in varying degrees of health, with an unstable relationship between body and mind' (Kirsten Brady, 'Thomas Hardy and Matters of Gender' in Kramer op. cit. p.97)

This organism is seen at its most primitive in Tess who was seen by many as morally pure precisely because she was physically impure, driven by her instincts towards an earthy sexuality, the nature of which was anathema to notions of Victorian womanhood. At the other extreme lies Sue Brideshead where morality and civilization have triumphed in what D. H. Lawrence described as a battleground between these forces and the primitive. Elizabeth Chapman had summed up this position most succinctly in her essay 'The Disparagement of Women in Literature' in describing Hardy's women as:

> … a compound three-parts animal and one part fey; or as one might put it, with *Jude* fresh in one's memory, three parts Arabella and one part Sue.

Brady characterizes the middle part of the last century as one in which Hardy was praised for his realistic depiction of Victorian women. Many critics commentated on his intuitive understanding and his ability to enter their emotional world and even that it was his love of women that gave him this special gift of verisimilitude.

The shift in the early 1970s away from such simplistic views coincided, not surprisingly, with the rise of **feminism** both as a political movement and as a critical perspective in

> **KEY TERM**
>
> Feminism: The study of gender politics from a female perspective. Usually the term is applied to the political and social movement which swept through Western Europe and the United States beginning in the late 1960s.

literature and the arts. Early feminist criticism is often formulated in terms of a vitriolic and polemic reaction to the comfortable patriarchal tradition summarized above. Widdowson includes one early piece by Jane Marcus which exemplifies the anger felt by many women at this period. In reviewing Polanski's film of *Tess* she comments on the director's failure to show the scene where Tess posthumously baptizes Sorrow, her illegitimate son:

> Polanski must have his reasons for failing to show this legendary scene. And the reason is that there is an unwritten rule against showing a woman justified in usurping a male power. Only a priest can baptize. And a priest has a penis.
>
> Marcus, J., 'A Tess for Child Molesters' reprinted in Widdowson (1981) op. cit. p.91

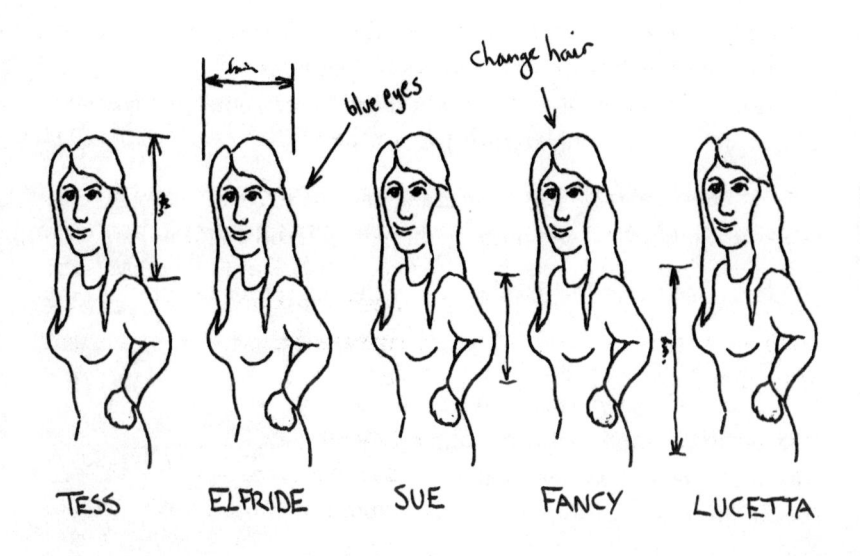

Hardy's heroines

VOYEURISM OF THE NARRATOR

Not surprisingly it is *Tess* that has attracted more feminist interest than other Hardy novels. It is the sexuality of Tess herself and the way that this is constructed within the novel which has been the focus of much recent academic attention. John Goode drew attention to the way in which Tess is made into an object for consumption by the reader. Equally Widdowson demonstrates that we are continually shown Tess by the way in which she is seen by others. We are given both Angel and Alec's view of her and on many occasions we are given by the narrator a highly voyeuristic portrait of Tess's physical form. Boumelha in her study of Hardy's women puts the case like this:

> And so it is that all the passionate commitment to exhibiting Tess as the subject of her own experience evokes an unusually overt maleness in the narrative voice. The narrator's erotic fantasies of penetration and engulfment enact a pursuit, violation and persecution of Tess in parallel with those she suffers at the hands of her two lovers.
>
> Boumelha, P., *Thomas Hardy and Women: Sexual Ideology and Narrative Form* (Harvester, 1982) p.120

She identifies many occasions within the story where the narrator seems to find ways of entering Tess's body through her eyes, her mouth and her flesh. This phallic imagery both links together Tess's experiences but also is seen by Boumelha as part of the narrator's fascination with Tess's sexuality, a fascination she suggests that extends as far as a desire to possess her entirely.

It is certainly possible to find many occasions within the text where physical aspects of Tess are **fetishistically** drawn to our attention, Here, for example, is Angel Clare observing her as she awakens:

> **KEY TERM**
>
> Fetish: An obsession, usually sexual, with a particular part of the body or aspect of human activity.

> She had not heard him enter, and hardly realized his presence there. She was yawning, and he saw

the red interior of her mouth as if it had been a snake's. She had stretched one arm so high above her coiled-up cable of hair that he could see its satin delicacy above the sunburn; her face was flushed with sleep, and her eyelids hung heavy over their pupils. The brimfulness of her nature breathed from her. It was a moment when a woman's soul is more incarnate than at any other time; when the most spiritual beauty bespeaks itself flesh; and sex takes the outside place in the presentation.

Tess of the d'Urbervilles, Chapter 27

The narrator seems to take us inside Tess's body, seeing her in a way that is intimate almost to the point of being uncomfortable.

STRUCTURALISM

Structuralism began with the work of Claude Levi Strauss (1908–) and Roland Barthes (1915–1980) and grew in importance in Britain in the early 1970s. As the name suggested it is concerned with structures and the notion that these structures can exist only in relation to one another. In essence, using the ideas of Swiss linguist Ferdinand de Saussure, structuralists stress the arbitrary nature of language. For example, a 'cow' in one language is a *vache* in another and a *kuh* in a third. The object remains the same, it is the word which changes. This has enormous implications for the way we understand language and the texts created with this language.

In literature one aspect of structuralism is concerned with seeing the parts of a play, poem or novel as part of a whole, and with finding the laws or rules which govern the structure of the whole text. As such it is more concerned with the form of the text rather than the content. Unlike more traditional critical methods structuralism is also not concerned about qualitative evaluation, as Terry Eagleton puts it in *Literary Theory: An Introduction*, 'anything from *War and Peace* to the *War Cry* will do' (Blackwells, 1996, p.83).

David Lodge's essay '*The Woodlanders*: A Darwinian Pastoral Elegy' can be seen, in part at least, as an exercise in structural analysis. The novel is compared to the classical Greek pastoral elegy.

The other influence Lodge suggests is that of Darwin:

> Like many thoughtful late Victorians, he [Hardy] was both an evolutionary and a pessimistic thinker: he believed in the inevitability of change without assuming that it would necessarily be change for the better.
>
> Lodge, D., *Working with Structuralism: Essays and Reviews on Nineteenth and Twentieth Century Literature* (Routledge, 1981) p.87

Lodge points to the pastoral references which lie at the heart of Hardy's novel, in particular the association of Giles Winterbourne with tradition and, most explicitly, with nature itself. There are numerous references to his harmony with trees and growth and many symbolic references to him as part of nature. The devotional mourning undertaken by both Grace and Marty upon Giles's death and the death itself both suggest the form of the pastoral elegy. As to the resolution of the plot, Lodge suggests it is split in two. Fitzpiers and Grace seek 'fresh woods, and pastures new' whilst Marty remains behind to nourish Giles's memory.

Lodge's essay combines fine and detailed attention to the text with a concern to understand the novel as a whole. He notes the oppositions in the text between the infiltrators such as Fitzpiers and Mrs Charmond and the woodlanders themselves, most notably Giles Winterbourne and Marty South. He notes the symbolism, for example, of the rape of Marty's locks by Percomb the barber or the death of John South when his tree is destroyed by Fitzpiers. Yet he also treats the novel as a whole in linking the literal and metaphoric elements of the story with those of the classical Greek pastoral elegy. It is this concern with the parts, which are seen as elements in the shape of the whole novel, that mark this approach as structuralist.

POST-STRUCTURALISM

Post-structuralism takes the structuralist proposition that it is language that shapes our world and considers the consequences of this radical idea. If our world is constructed by language then maybe it is not as tangible as we would like to imagine. Where are the certainties, the fixed points, that can help us work out where we are, even who we are? The post-structuralists refer to a world that is uncertain and unknown as the **decentred universe**.

KEY TERM

Decentred universe: A universe where there are no fixed certainties, no absolutes. Everything is relative and so only definable in terms of something else which in itself lacks any degree of certainty.

Possibly because of all this uncertainty, post-structuralist criticism is quite difficult to understand. It is also hard to find an approach which can be seen as definitively post-structuralist. The plurality of post-modernist criticism means that most academics are influenced by a range of different approaches and, quite rightly, often object to being seen as representative of a particular school of thought. Certainly, however, Ramón Saldívar's essay, '*Jude The Obscure*: Reading and the Spirit of the Law' is highly influenced by post-structuralist thinking.

Saldívar looks at the problems of reading and interpreting *Jude*, bearing in mind Hardy's often incensed claims that his intentions in writing the book were so frequently misinterpreted by his critics. Saldívar suggests that Jude, too, has a propensity for misreading, for instance Jude's belief that the process of translation from one language to another is dependent on a cipher, a code, the possession of which will transmute words from Latin or Greek into English. Jude, he asserts is continually misreading his world. He creates an illusionary Christminster, idealizes Phillotson out of all recognition, gets Arabella completely wrong and as for Sue:

> When Jude looks into Sue's 'untranslatable eyes' (II ii) and immediately begins to interpret her character, he is only repeating the established pattern of error.
>
> Reprinted in Bouhelma, P., *New Casebook: Jude The Obscure*
> (Macmillan, 2000) p.34

All of these are constructed by Jude into an inaccessible but ideal paradise. It is as if Jude is continually attempting to create a world which does not exist. Jude's dreams are transmuted from one to the other. He expresses a desire to impose order into his world. Saldívar suggests that while we as readers can in retrospect see an order in the narrative, Jude's attempts within the tale as it unfolds to understand this order must continuously fail.

Saldívar suggests the following schema for the complex structures of the novel:

(1) dreams that fail – Jude, Phillotson, Sue;
(2) marriages that fail – Jude and Arabella; Sue and Phillotson; Jude and Sue; Arabella and Cartlett; both sets of parents; the legendary ancestor;
(3) returns to original failures – Jude and Arabella at Christminster; Sue and Phillotson at Marygreen.

ibid. p.39

Saldívar reminds us that Hardy referred to the 'geometric structure' of *Jude*. Yet what has happened here is a reversal. Jude and Arabella began at Marygreen while Sue and Phillotson began at Christminster. For Saldívar this is a *chiasmus*, which means a diagonal or cross-wise arrangement. Rather than be returned to their original places as a geometrical construction would suggest, the couples are reversed. This structure lies at the heart of the story, as well as representing the themes of the novel and the relationships of the central characters.

LACK OF CONSENSUS

One characteristic of contemporary writing on Hardy is a lack of consensus. Robert Schweik in his essay 'Less Than Faithfully Presented: Fictions in Modern Commentaries on Hardy's *Tess*' questions a number of modern interpretations of *Tess*. He finds some of these both tangential and remote. He accuses some academics of creating a fictional version of Tess far removed from the one presented to us by Hardy. Among others he identifies those who treat Tess as though she were a character who can exist independently of her author:

...they have imaginatively endowed her with a 'secret being' that 'the novel never attempts to penetrate', with a specific sexuality that Hardy is unable to construe correctly, and with a 'point of view' that Hardy cannot comprehend.

from Pettit, Charles P. C., *Reading Thomas Hardy*

(Macmillan, 1998) p.36

Post-modernist criticism is certainly not a place to seek certainty or even necessarily clarity. Leavis and the New Critics in the 1950s and 60s are much easier if all that is required is a definitive reading of a text. The broad range of approaches that make up post-modernism challenge any notion of a single reading of a text, or that there is a 'right' way of seeing a particular text. Whether Schweik is correct that many of these readings are so far removed from the original text as to be fictions themselves remains to be seen. Certainly the post-structuralists would argue that ambiguity is part of the way in which language is constructed: criticism cannot therefore give us answers, it can only encourage us to ask questions. Ambiguity can only be analysed, it cannot be eliminated.

✳ ✳ ✳ ✳SUMMARY ✳ ✳ ✳ ✳

- Hardy was highly sensitive to the negative criticism he received from some of his contemporaries.

- Hardy anticipated some of the concerns of the Modernists, although his work cannot be considered part of that movement.

- Leavis and other poets of the mid-twentieth century were dismissive of Hardy.

- Hardy has always remained popular with readers.

- Feminist readings of his work have been critical of many of his heroines.

- Structuralist and post-structuralist critics have found new meanings in his work.

Where to Next?

9

HARDY'S OTHER PROSE

It is fascinating to read all Hardy's novels in chronological order of writing. You will then get an idea not only of his development but also of his range. *Desperate Remedies*, for example, his first novel, is in the genre of detective fiction and very different from his other works.

The short stories have a different flavour, often more firmly embedded in the history and myth of rural Wessex. They are tales concerning the threat of invasion, smuggling, hanging, death, superstition and other rural concerns. Some of these are collected together as *Wessex Tales* and are widely available.

HARDY'S POETRY

The poetry is very popular and all of it is still in print today. The full works are obtainable inexpensively as *The Works of Thomas Hardy* (Wordsworth Poetry Library, 1994). Penguin Books publish a representative and well-respected collection, assembled in 1978 but still in print called *Thomas Hardy Selected Poetry*. As a useful companion guide, you can obtain the excellent *Thomas Hardy's Poetry*, a study guide written by John Ward (Open University, 1993). It refers to poems in the Penguin edition.

VISUAL MEDIA

Hardy translates well to film, probably because his techniques of describing landscape and the people in it are film-like in nature. Apart from many classic film versions, television also adapts Hardy's novels on a regular basis. *Far From the Madding Crowd* directed by John Schlesinger in 1967 is something of a classic as is the Roman Polanski *Tess* made in 1979. The 1996 adaptation of *Jude* starring Kate Winslet is also worth watching.

BIOGRAPHY AND BACKGROUND

The fullest biography, and the one to refer to on factual matters is *Thomas Hardy: A Biography* by Michael Millgate, plus the two volumes by Robert Gittings *The Young Thomas Hardy* and *The Older Hardy*. A third biography by Martin Seymour-Smith is simply called *Hardy*. A shorter biography, of particular interest to students, is *Thomas Hardy* by James Gibson in the Macmillan (Palgrave) 'Literary Lives' series. A useful book is Hardy's *Life*, written ostensibly by Florence Emily but actually by Hardy himself.

CRITICAL THEORY

There is a fast-growing body of work about Hardy. The following are good places to begin:

Penny Boumelha, *New Casebook: Jude the Obscure* (Macmillan, 2000)
Timothy Hands, *Writers in Their Time: Thomas Hardy* (Macmillan, 1995)
Barbara Hardy, *Thomas Hardy* (The Athlone Press, 2000)
Michael Irwin, *Reading Hardy's Landscapes* (Macmillan, 2000)
Dale Kramer, *The Cambridge Companion to Thomas Hardy* (CUP, 1999)
John Powell Ward, *Thomas Hardy's Poetry* (OUP, 1993)
Peter Widdowson, *New Casebook: Tess of the d'Urbervilles* (Macmillan, 1993)

ASSOCIATIONS

The Thomas Hardy Association (TTHA) exists to promote the study and appreciation of Hardy's writings in every corner of the world. It maintains for its members an Internet site, with departments focusing on Hardy's life and work, and with links to other sites of possible interest to Hardy lovers. TTHA promotes interchanges among its members by supporting a Forum discussion group, a Poem-of-the-Month page, a *Hardy Review*, and a page featuring student papers. Application for membership to TTHA can be made through the website.

The website is available to all and is a mine of information. The address is: http://www.yale.edu/hardysoc

Linked to the TTHA is the Thomas Hardy Society. Through it you can obtain *The Thomas Hardy Journal*, a UK publication issued three times a year free to members. Applications for membership should be made to: The Thomas Hardy Society. PO Box 1438, Dorchester, Dorset DTI IYH, England.

DORSET HARDY COLLECTION

The Dorset County Museum houses the world's finest Thomas Hardy collection and in July 1997 opened new galleries about Thomas Hardy and other Dorset writers. The exhibit includes paintings, photographs, drawings, letters and other materials – along with original manuscripts of some of Hardy's greatest works.

At the time of writing, the galleries are open from 10 am to 5 pm Monday to Saturday, and also on Sundays in July and August. The research collections may be viewed by prior appointment.

HARDY COUNTRY

Many pleasurable hours can be spent in Hardy's Wessex, visiting his house at Max Gate, just outside Dorchester, and exploring the countryside associated with the writing. Max Gate is open on Sunday, Monday and Wednesday from 2 pm to 5 pm, April to September.

✴✴✴✴SUMMARY ✴✴✴✴

- Read and watch Hardy's work.

- Study his biography and background.

- Read some critical theory about him.

- Join an association.

- Visit the THHA website.

- Visit the Hardy collection at Dorset County Museum.

- Explore Hardy country.

Glossary

Affective   Having an emotion-influencing effect.

Ballad   A traditional form, based originally in song and dance, which tells a story. A literary type developed which stood without musical accompaniment, although it kept its metrical form.

Bowdlerize   To publish an expurgated version of a text. A term derived from the activities of Thomas Bowdler who published heavily cut versions of Shakespeare's plays.

Canon   The authentic works of a writer. A term often used to mean the full range of that work. It is also used to describe the full range of a group of writers, or literature as a whole.

Courtship plot   The most basic of all stories: boy meets girl and, after overcoming a series of obstacles, they marry.

Decentred universe   A universe where there are no fixed certainties, no absolutes. Everything is relative and so only ever definable in terms of something else which in itself lacks any degree of certainty.

Elegy   A poem of mourning in reflective mode, as in Thomas Grays's 'Elegy Written in a Country Churchyard' Alfred Lord Tennyson's 'In Memoriam' and G.M. Hopkins's 'The Wreck of the Deutschland'.

An **eponymous** hero or heroine is one whose name appears in the title of the work e.g. *Don Juan, Robinson Crusoe, The Mayor of Casterbridge.*

Fatalism   The belief that all things are determined by fate.

Feminism   The study of gender politics from a female perspective. Usually the term is applied to the political and social movement which swept through Western Europe and the United States beginning in the late 1960s.

Fetish   An obsession, usually sexual with a particular part of the body or aspect of human activity.

Georgian poetry   A term now used pejoratively to refer to the worst of poetry written in the early part of the last century. Such poetry is much criticized for its pastoral and escapist style.

Incubus   An evil spirit supposed to descend upon sleeping people, and often to have sexual intercourse with sleeping women. Belief in these evil creatures was widespread: indeed, the existence of such incubi was recognized by law in Medieval times.

Many women claimed that their illegitimate children were the result of rape by an incubus.

Luddites   Followers of Ned Lud who in 1811–16 went about destroying machinery, particularly in the Midlands and the North, in protest about the loss of jobs and lowering of pay which accompanied their introduction.

Melodrama   A play form that was highly popular with Victorian audiences. It was characterized by sensationalism and the battle of good against evil. It had a powerful influence upon the popular Victorian novels as well as the work of serious novelists such as Hardy and Dickens.

Modernism   In literarature, a broad movement of writers including T.S. Eliot, Pound, Joyce, Woolf, Yeats and D.H. Lawrence. It was informed by the works of Freud and was characterized by a persistent experimentation with language and form. Stream of consciousness is one of its major techniques as well as dependence upon poetic image and myth.

New Woman fiction   The New Woman movement of the 1890s sought individual and social freedoms for women, including: a rejection of marriage; a more honest approach to female sexuality; and a demand for more economic and personal independence. New Woman fiction explored some of these issues, some books becoming best sellers, most notably, Sarah Grand's *The Heavenly Twins*, George Egerton's *Keynotes*, and Grant Allen's *The Woman Who Did*. The movement was eclipsed by the suffragists who sought equality through the ballot box, rather than through personal and sexual freedom.

Pantheism   The notion that God is everything and everywhere.

Realism   A style, otherwise known as social realism, best illustrated in English writing at least by the works of authors such as Bennett and Galsworthy. Precise definition is almost impossible but the general idea is that what is represented in the literature is seen in some way like what might be found in the world that it strives to represent.

Romanticism   A movement in Britain and Europe roughly between 1770 and 1848. In literary terms it emphasized self-expression and the value of individual experience, along with a strong sense of the transcendental. The motif of the movement was 'imagination' and it put forward a belief in the close links between Man and Nature. The movement is characterized by such writers as Rousseau, Wordsworth, Mary Wollstonecraft, Coleridge, Byron and Shelley.

Symbolism, or more properly **symbolism** (with a small 's'), is the use of one image or concept to represent another. In Hardy, the weather is often used to symbolize mood. In the first chapter of *The Return of the Native* Hardy's complex descriptions of landscape and weather symbolize the psychological territory his characters will inhabit within the narrative.

Synaesthesia   In this context, a metaphor where an effect produced by stimulating all the senses suggests other states.

Theory   something of a 'catch all' term which is applied to the wave-like succession of new approaches to literature beginning in the 1970s. The term 'literary theory' is frequently used, but 'theory' captures the multi-disciplinary nature of these movements.

Chronology of major works

INDEX